JESUS BREAKS THE CHAINS

"One Man's Journey into The Captivity, Darkness, and Hell of Addiction and Deliverance Back to his God"

Written By:

MICHAEL BOWEN

PSALM 107:10-16 (NKJV)
Those who sat in darkness and in the shadow of death, bound in affliction and irons because they rebelled against the words of God, and despised the counsel of the Most High, therefore He brought down their heart with labor; they fell down, and there was none to help. Then they cried out to the LORD in their trouble, and He saved them out of their distresses. He brought them out of darkness and the shadow of death, and **BROKE THEIR CHAINS** in pieces. Oh, that men would give thanks to the LORD for His goodness, and for His wonderful works to the children of men! For He has broken the gates of bronze, and cut the bars of iron in two.

Copyright © 2025 by Michael Bowen

All rights reserved. No part of this publication may be reproduced, distributed, or transmitted in any form or by any means, including photocopying, recording, or other electronic or mechanical methods, without the prior written permission of the author/publisher. For permission requests, please contact the author.

THIS BOOK IS A WITNESS AND TESTIMONY TO MY LORD AND SAVIOR JESUS CHRIST, FOR WITHOUT HIM I AM STILL LOST, AND THIS BOOK DOES NOT EXIST...

A heartfelt thank you and unending love to my parents, sisters, children, and loved ones. I understand it was a long, tough, and challenging journey filled with tears and many glorious peaks and low-lying dark valleys, but look at us—we made it!

A special thanks to my friends who stuck by my side through the good, the bad, and the ugly. You know who you are, and you are more than just friends—you are my brothers and sisters for life!

Thank you to all the prison ministers who visited me in prison and introduced me to my God. Without you, I would not have discovered the truth that has set me free!

To all my ministry partners in Texas and Liberia, I love you all, and we are in this fight together to destroy the works of the devil and to be laborers in the harvest for souls. We are soldiers for Christ in the advancement of God's Kingdom here on earth. It is an honor to work with you and stand side by side in this fight—I got you!

Finally, this book is dedicated to all of you who are still fighting through the captivity, darkness, and hell of addiction. Keep your head up and your eyes fixed on Jesus, and the light of the world will lead your way to freedom.

This book is written in loving memory of those who have left this world and are gone but not forgotten: Aunt Ramona Napier, Aunt Elizabeth Walters, Grandaddy Ramon Bowen, Mu-Mu Virginia Bowen, Guy-Boy Guy Graves, Me-Maw Alta Mae Graves, Scott Huckabay, Mike Gaar, Jill Gaar, Marty Kidd, Jim Larsen, Travis Preston, Mario Greene OG, Addie Mae Lee, Bruce Bingham, Tee Augustine Dorbor, and DeDe Waggoner.

"YOU WIN THE WAR ON DRUGS ONE SOUL AT A TIME"

TABLE OF CONTENTS

FORWARD vi

INTRODUCTION 1

I. HOW DID I DIE? 9

II. MY ADDICTION 15

III. MUSTANG PRIDE 81

IV. DEEP IN THE HEART OF TEXAS 101

V. CAPTURED BY GOD 109

VI. SHINE 143

VII. MY HOLY WAR ON ADDICTION 157

FORWARD

It's an honor to write these words for a brother from another mother, a friend, and a ministry partner. Our lives, divinely crossing paths, continue to bring out the best in our respective callings and ministries. We plant together, water together, and wait together for the increase of souls being won to Christ through our ministry efforts.

Paul's description of his life's work in the phrase "...this one thing I do..." vividly illustrates the life of Evangelist Michael Bowen. He is a man on a single mission: the liberation of drug addicts (Zogos, as they are called in Liberia) from the chains of addiction through the power of Jesus Christ. He lives, eats, sleeps, and dreams of "Zogo Liberation."

This book details his work among Zogos in Liberia, reflecting his 25-year battle with drugs. Growing up in a world where he believed he had it all—family wealth, a good education, being a star college football player, and getting drafted to play professional football—he was at the height of success. From the peaks of fame and achievement, he plummeted into the depths of crack cocaine addiction, imprisonment, and near-death experiences. His journey through addiction, incarceration, and close calls with death led him to meet Jesus, the only one able to deliver him from the chains of addiction.

This book is a gem for anyone struggling with addiction or for those who have connections with individuals facing addiction. It answers the question of an ultimate solution to the devastating problem of drug addiction. If there was ever any doubt about finding a permanent solution to the issue of drug addiction, this book offers that permanent solution. Read it with an open heart and be blessed by its pages. Jesus breaks the chains!

Blessings,
Samuel M. Nunoo

INTRODUCTION

Jesus Breaks the Chains was conceived on the very first day of my teenage years. I believed the enemy's lie that alcohol and drugs could be trusted. It was born in fiery revelation 30 years later, behind bars in a Texas prison, by the power of the Holy Spirit, after God reached into my fallen life and delivered me out of the captivity, darkness, and hell of addiction into the loving arms of my Lord and Savior Jesus Christ. In a raging battle with alcoholism and drug addiction for more than two-thirds of my life, at age 46, I had fallen so fast and so deep into addicted darkness that up until that time, I had never experienced anything like it before. As a man who had just completed his first time in prison and was beginning a new life in my home state of Texas, I thought the days of disappearing into the very dangerous and unpredictable world of crack cocaine and methamphetamine addiction were behind me. Boy, was I wrong!

Addiction controlled my life for 25 years, leading to a roller coaster ride of instability, chaos, and destruction. My journey through addiction was a dangerous escape into the harsh, unforgiving world of addiction. It was an intense inward journey into myself and back out, which ultimately transformed me into the Man of God I am today. Looking back, I see a landscape marked by towering mountains of achievement, filled with success and praise, alongside dark valleys of collapse, characterized by loneliness and despair. I experienced phases of great success, only to be met with tragic failure, then clawed my way back to the top of a mountain and somehow found prosperity again. Once I reached these new heights, I would, like clockwork, be unable to stay there and would fall again into failure, tumbling into the emotionally hostile terrain of guilt, shame, frustration, and disappointment.

This book offers an in-depth look at how addiction entered my life and took root in my soul early on. As an unsuspecting, naive, and unprepared teen experimenting with alcohol and drugs, I believed the lie that these substances could be friends I could trust to provide harmless fun and excitement. I thought they would bring endless good times with no negative effects or consequences. Let the good times roll, and let the party never end! That was the bait, and addiction was the trap.

Growing up in Dallas, Texas, during the late 1970s and 1980s, I was the only son in a family that was well-educated, successful in business, and attended church on Sundays. I was also a highly talented athlete, which propelled me to become a well-known and successful high school and college football player, earning many honors and accolades. My addiction erupted in my life in 1991, the year I was cut from the Edmonton Eskimos Football Team in the Canadian Football League. Like a dormant volcano suddenly blowing its top, I was propelled headfirst into the crack cocaine epidemic that raged in our country's inner cities and ghettos across the country. For a young man raised with wealth, fame, and a solid education, this experience was a stark contrast to the beautiful university campus and the wealthy suburban neighborhoods where I once lived and played. This book offers a deep look into my profound and tragic descent into the wickedness of addiction. It describes in detail the unbelievable destruction this destructive force caused in every area and relationship of my life. Addiction, with its sharp, piercing hooks, latched onto me, embedding itself deep into my flesh and soul, refusing to let go. I was hooked. I was trapped. Unknowingly, I was headed straight for hell. You will read about my journey into darkness and the shadow of death, and my final encounter with the devil himself when he asked for my soul.

While taking on a life of its own, addiction led me into a vast emotional wilderness filled with pain, misery, disgust, defeat, anguish, and disappointment. These experiences marked my soul with several illuminating spiritual awakenings and revelations that I will share throughout this book. The deeper I traveled into this maze of insanity and the longer I walked the dark, lonely road toward destruction, the more I realized I was caught in a crossfire of a battle being fought for my very soul. The overwhelming suffering caused by my level of addiction became the fuel that eventually brought me back to my

God. The lie of addiction and the spiritual sickness that comes with it became the enemy's weapon to attack me, aiming to destroy my soul and trick me into following him into the pits of hell reserved for him and the fallen angels who rebelled against God. The enemy used addiction to drive me into rebellion against my Creator. His plan was to separate me and keep me disconnected from the Light, Love, and Truth of my Lord and Savior Jesus Christ, who instead became my saving Grace and Rescuer. Through His incredible Power and endless Love, Jesus faithfully lifted me out of the lies and deceptions that formed the dark pit of addiction, delivering me into the fullness of His Spirit of Truth.

Jesus Breaks the Chains testifies that when Jesus sets you free, you are truly free. I hold this truth: when a drug addict surrenders everything to the Lord, only then can they be transformed through the power of the Holy Spirit and the authority in the name of Jesus Christ, ultimately stepping into victory over all addictions—just as Jesus Christ has victory over all things. After I surrendered to Jesus Christ and chose life, I entered into a personal, loving relationship with Him and found rest for my tired, battle-worn soul. When I made Jesus Christ the Lord and Savior of my life, that decision declared His victory over my addiction. In Jesus Christ, I have finally discovered my integrity through my Spirit-guided life of action and obedience to God's Word. The Lord has led me out of the cycle of defeat into the triumph of victory, something I have only experienced in Him. I am successful when I stop trying to be my own god and savior, stop following the world's broken beliefs, and fully surrender my will to the will of my Creator, Jesus Christ.

As I submit myself and my will to the Lord of my life, He guides me into His understanding and His wisdom about the person He created me to be. In this, He reveals to me His purpose for my life. As He shares His truth with me, as long as I remain submitted to His will, I am open to becoming that person—a new creation, a disciple, and a witness of Jesus Christ. As God completes His good work in me and begins the process of transforming me into the image of His Son, I can understand God's purpose for my life. Once I discover my purpose, I can start living it out, cooperating with God in His plan. Then my life begins to make sense, the inner struggle ends, and I find peace.

2 CORINTHIANS 5:17 (NKJV)

Therefore, if anyone is in Christ, he is a new creation; old things have passed away; behold, all things have become new.

In Jesus Christ, all old things have passed away, including my addiction and the wreckage of my past. Now, all things are new, and I can rest in the assurance that Jesus can do better for me than I can ever do for myself alone. I get out of my own way and let God have His way in me. As I do this, God creates in me a new life, guided by His gentle, loving, yet firm hand, as He leads me into all truth. My hope is for full healing in all my current relationships, which are truly precious to me, and for understanding, forgiveness, and restoration in the relationships that were broken in my past. I am humble, contrite, remorseful, and apologetic for all the hurt and pain I caused others during my addiction and for the damage it did to the people I loved most. I seize every opportunity that God provides to make amends to those people. My new way of life and walk in the Spirit will serve as a witness and testimony to everyone about the truth in Jesus Christ, our Lord and Savior, and that through Him, all things are possible, including victory over addiction. The most important thing in my life, rising from the ashes of a cold, addicted death, is my relationship with Jesus Christ and my life's mission to share His Love, Hope, and Strength with others so they too can escape the land of the lost, the land of the living dead, and join me in the Triumph of Jesus Christ over addiction.

Please enjoy the story of my life and God's poetry given to me in fiery revelation from behind the bars of a cold, lonely, and depressing prison in Austin, Texas, USA. During my incarceration, I finally surrendered to Jesus Christ, listened to God's voice, and followed

His life-giving instructions, which led me happily to freedom. In Jesus Christ, I have broken free from the heavy yoke and stifling bondage of self. I claim victory in Jesus Christ over the addiction that nearly destroyed my soul. I have escaped a world gone insane and been delivered from my stubborn, rebellious, and sinful fleshly nature, which, until now, held me captive and imprisoned in darkness for most of my life. I have now settled into the rest and peace of my Lord and Savior, Jesus Christ. The Prince of Peace led me into freedom, in the most unlikely place on this planet to find liberty. I found sweet freedom as a five-time convicted felon, locked in a sad and lonely prison behind razor wire fences, steel doors, and rough concrete walls. It was in this prison that I was finally able to break through the biggest lie of my life—the enemy's weapon of addiction in a war being waged for the destiny of my soul between the forces of good and evil. Because of my surrender to Jesus Christ, I have been delivered back to my God, out of a horrible, drug-addicted pit, by His saving grace and mercy, incomprehensible, unfailing love, and the incredible power and truth that can only be found in a relationship with my Lord and Savior Jesus Christ.

I hope that you, who are reading this book, will invite Jesus Christ into your heart through the story of my life, the poetry of my soul, and the scripture written in this book. I pray that the Holy Spirit reveals to you in your spirit the fiery truth about addiction and who Jesus Christ is as our Lord and Savior, the only begotten Son of our Father, Almighty God! Whether you are struggling with addiction or simply an interested reader, this book is my deepest expression to you—honestly sharing my lifelong battle with addiction and my final deliverance from it into the truth. Today, I stand with absolute authority, firmly and boldly over addiction, with my foot pressing squarely on its neck, and I proclaim fearlessly the victorious battle cry of Victory given to me by the Power of the Blood and the authority in the Name of Jesus Christ.

We all must embark on our own personal journey through the trials and tribulations of this fallen, dark, and deceptive world. Along the way, we are challenged to break free from the grip of sin and death and step into the Light of eternal life with our Creator. My journey led me through some of the most dangerous, spiritually wicked wildernesses and wastelands of the living dead, winding through dark valleys of alcohol, crack cocaine, and methamphetamine addiction, ending in a devastating pit of defeat, despair, and an encounter with the devil. Your journey may be similar or different, but it is unique to you and your own. Wherever your path takes you, I wish you Godspeed, and I hope the story of my life, as shared in this book, will inspire and encourage you to never give up. It took me over 20 years to finally conquer my flesh, the devil, addiction, and my bondage to sin. No matter how many times you fall, you must get back up, keep fighting, and cry out to Jesus for help. Remember, victory over your life, addiction, and sin only comes when you surrender completely to the loving care of Jesus Christ. Surrendering my life to Jesus removed the endless, unsuccessful, and often defeated battle from my own hands—hands too weak to withstand the test of time—and placed the fight in the powerful, unending strength, authority, and dominion of Jesus Christ, who has victory over all things. Our victory has already been won, and Jesus waits for us to enforce it by accepting Him. I finally exhausted my strength and stepped into Christ's power, embracing and applying His victory to my life. This only happened when I surrendered every part of myself—what was good, bad, and ugly—to Him. In my deepest brokenness and destruction, I was able to surrender fully, and immediately, I entered into the peace of His victory, finding much-needed rest for my tormented, weary, downtrodden, and battle-worn soul. As I made a complete white-flag surrender to Jesus, I entered into His truth, righteousness, and the fullness of His unconditional love. Not by my own limited strength or understanding—ill-equipped to handle such overwhelming chaos—only through the power, wisdom, and grace of the Most High God, the Creator of all things, was I able to finally overcome my addiction.

1 JOHN 5:4-5 (NKJV)

For whatever is born of God overcomes the world. And this is the victory that has overcome the world—our faith. Who is he who overcomes the world but he who believes that Jesus is the Son of God?

Read this book, and if you relate to any part of it, then you, too, can triumph over any addiction or difficulty that keeps you in bondage and prevents you from being your best and living a life of freedom and prosperity. My victory, found only in Jesus Christ, comes from the Lord, who gave me the mission and calling of my life: to proclaim to all who will listen the good news of the Gospel of Jesus Christ and to expose the lie of addiction so others can be set free as I have been.

The Lord has rescued me from drug addiction and imprisonment. He has called me to the mission field, leading me back into the Texas prison system and also overseas to drug-infested communities and prisons in Liberia, West Africa. There, I help the brokenhearted, drug-addicted, despised, and rejected prisoners of sin, guilt, and shame. In Monrovia, Liberia's capital, drug-addicted men, women, and young people have taken over Palm Grove Cemetery and the nearby Center Street Ghetto. This cemetery spans nearly 13 acres and is home to over 1,500 tombs. Fourteen years of civil war, fought with machetes, left many bodies buried. Some older drug addicts are former child soldiers and abuse victims from this brutal war who turned to drugs and had nowhere else to go afterward. Warlords kidnapped young boys and often murdered their family members in front of them before forcing them into battle. To make the frightened children fight, the warlords supplied them with drugs to make them brave, which led to addiction. They handed out marijuana, crack cocaine, black tar heroin, and a mixture called Cane Juice—alcohol, cane juice, and gunpowder—that intoxicated them and was said to make them fearless. Warlords even forced children to cannibalize victims and drink the blood of sacrificed children. Once disarmament occurred, the government confiscated guns and machetes, but the addiction and trauma persisted. The devastating civil wars planted the seed of drug addiction in Liberia.

Today, people of all ages from multiple generations are addicted to drugs and living in graveyards and ghettos across the country under terrible conditions. Babies are being born into this environment and are never given a fair chance at a decent life. The infant mortality rate is high. This suffering group is called Zogos. They have been forgotten and persecuted by society, even unto death. Very few resources are available to help the Zogos. These hurt, broken, lost, and addicted people need our help. Praise the Lord! God has given me this ministry, a burden, and a massive mission to serve the drug-addicted, poor, homeless, and disadvantaged people of Liberia! We are here to show them that Jesus has not forgotten them, and neither have we. I have established a nonprofit 501(c)(3) organization in the United States called Sons and Daughters of Thunder Ministries, along with a Liberian NGO called Liberation Center Liberia, to support this calling in my life. What Jesus did in me, He will do in those I am sent to serve as a witness of His endless grace, mercy, and love!

ZECHARIAH 4:6 (NKJV)

'Not by might nor by power, but by My Spirit,' says the Lord of hosts.

The same Spirit that hovered over the face of the waters at creation and the same Spirit that raised Jesus from the dead is the same Spirit that dwells in me and anoints me for this mission and calling to help God transform the lives of the drug-addicted and habitually incarcerated. It is this same Spirit that everyone who surrenders their life to Jesus Christ receives when they are born again and becomes the righteousness of God, overcoming their addictions and sins to become new creations in Jesus Christ, just as I have. I am a living example of what is possible with God. My life testifies to His goodness!

"May God bless you when reading this book and give you a new revelation and understanding of your Victory over all things that can only be found in Jesus Christ." ~ Michael Bowen

I. HOW DID I DIE?

PSALM 139:8 (KJV)
If I ascend up into heaven, thou art there: if I make my bed in hell, behold, thou art there.

MATTHEW 13:49-50 (NIV)
This is how it will be at the end of the age. The angels will come and separate the wicked from the righteous and throw them into the blazing furnace, where there will be weeping and gnashing of teeth.

PSALM 49:12-14 (NIV)
People, despite their wealth, do not endure; they are like the beasts that perish. This is the fate of those who trust in themselves, and of their followers, who approve their sayings. They are like sheep and are destined to die; death will be their shepherd (but the upright will prevail over them in the morning). Their forms will decay in the grave, far from their princely mansions.

It's March 2013, and I am sitting in a crack house in the deepest, darkest pit of addicted hell, entirely convinced that I have fallen so far and so deep that I can never return to the life I once had. I have run away from and abandoned what most people would consider a "good life." I have been missing for several weeks, and no one knows my whereabouts. I have been smoking crack every day nonstop without eating or much sleep. The devil has convinced me that I am hated and despised by everyone I know and love because I have done something so terrible and despicable. Now, this drug house has become my new home, and smoking crack feels like the only life I have left. I have completely shut myself off from reality, and the constant flow of crack into my system has become my only desire. I have forsaken my three children, my loved ones, my close friends, all my responsibilities, and the boys I coach in football and track.

One evening, a few weeks earlier, on a weekday, I went out for a few drinks at the bar and planned to go home afterward. Instead, I found myself caught in the dangerous grip of a crack house that refused to let me go. Now, the crack cocaine, mixed with overwhelming fear, shame, and guilt, has me held captive in a dark, wicked, and deceptive drug den. I left my safe, comfortable home where my children were sleeping, fully intending to return after a couple of drinks, but I never made it home that night. The alcohol I was drinking wasn't strong enough to numb the emptiness, loneliness, and emotional pain I'd always buried deep inside for reasons I didn't understand. The steady flow of drinks couldn't untangle the confusion in my mind about why I couldn't find joy in a life full of good things. The alcohol did not ease the suffocating stress gripping my soul, so I searched for something much stronger. I drove around the neighborhood for a while and finally found the friend I was looking for. Boom, and once again, I disappeared into the dark, wicked, and unpredictable world of crack cocaine.

I have been smoking crack nonstop for a couple of weeks, sitting in a dark room of a crack house where people come from the streets to buy and smoke crack. It's called a trap house because once you're caught in this trap, there's no way out! I am hiding in terror from the reality of what I've done, knowing my life will never be the same. A paralyzing fear overtakes me as I agonize over my situation, staring into a darkness I've never seen before. Confusion hits me, pushing me deeper into the abyss. I am falling so fast with no chance to stop into this nasty, stinking, selfish, pitiful hole I have pridefully dug for myself once again. This time, I can't even remember ever going this far into wickedness—falling so deep into the dark pit of addiction so quickly, with no way out. I am slowly losing myself to the evil madness that's stealing everything good left inside me. I fight hard to hold on to memories of my old life, but they drift further and further away into the breaking distance of my mind. Like sand slipping through my tight fists, the memories fall away sadly, leaving me only with this crack house that's become my home and my insatiable craving for more drugs to escape my worst nightmare. As the weight of my haunting reality presses down and unbearable stress claws at my soul, a heavy darkness settles over me as something unseen in the room shifts. Then, there's a knock at the door!

The door opens as I struggle to adjust to these strange, unfamiliar surroundings and the darkness that seems to consume my entire being. The door swings open, revealing a scruffy, disheveled old man with hauntingly piercing blue eyes peeking through his filthy, matted hair as he enters the room. He looks like he crawled out from a dirt hole under an abandoned bridge. He sits in the chair to my right and begins to smoke crack. He lights his pipe, inhaling deeply from his hit of crack, while I observe him in my peripheral vision, then watch as he exhales wicked smoke into the air. Then he starts to speak. As he begins talking, I immediately feel this tormenting presence start to gnaw at me, biting deep within my soul.

Quickly, I become unsettled and agitated as a vicious, dark, evil force grips me, and I start to gnash my teeth uncontrollably. Listening to him speak, I cannot understand what he is saying. I am frozen now in absolute fear, and the torment intensifies as it becomes clear to me that this man has something demonic inside him. He speaks very quickly and forms complete sentences, but once I hear them, I understand all the words, although they are out of order, and it sounds like complete gibberish. It's as if something is taking his words after they leave his mouth and rearranging them in the air before they reach my ear. As he continues to speak, I find myself unable to decipher his foreign, devilish tongue. His words are a wicked code flowing from the darkness of hell into my consciousness. I feel myself falling and drowning in a sea of torment, unable to stop the grinding and gnashing of my teeth. My body begins to feel like it is on fire, and I suddenly whisper in horror, "Oh my God, how did I die? Oh my God, I have died, and I am in hell! Oh my God, how did I die?" Still gnashing my teeth and burning with heat, I frantically look around the room, convinced that I have died and this crack house is my never-ending hell. "Oh my God, how did I die?"

My mind and body begin to sizzle with a burning fire, and in a panic, still gnashing my teeth violently, my eyes dart around the room as I struggle to catch a glimpse of anything that will make sense to me and tell me that this isn't true. All I recognize is what I perceive to be my everlasting hell. "Oh my God, how did I die?" The more I say to myself, "This can't be real", the more I believe that it is. I finally accept that I am now dead and in some bizarre, strange hell, lost forever in its tormenting shadow of death. This has now become my reality. I am convinced without any doubt that I have somehow died in a crack house and my soul is trapped here for eternity. I try to remember the event that caused my death, thinking that maybe I had overdosed or someone had shot me, and I began checking my body for bullet holes. "Where was I shot?" I am stricken with panic and cannot remember my death, so I start to say to myself like a broken record in utter grieving defeat, 'How did I die? How did I die? How did I die?" I then begin bargaining with myself in desperation, saying, "I know I was alive, but somehow, I must have died when the room changed, and I fell into this purgatory. Please, Lord, do not let this be my drug-addicted hell forever! Please, Lord, do not let this be!" I want to remember my death so I can come to terms with my new reality, and I try with all of my might to recall the events, but every stream of questioning thought always runs into a wall, a dead end that leaves me stranded, saying to myself once again, "How did I die?" In final demoralizing agonizing utter defeat, with all the life drained out of me and the realization that I have lost my soul to the devil and now have to spend eternity in this crack house hell, I say to myself, "My poor children."

Looking back now on that nightmare, I cannot fully describe using words the sheer terror, absolute horror, and agonizing defeat that encapsulated this devastating moment where I thought I had died and gone to hell. This was the first and only time in my life when all the fight I ever had was sucked out of me. I finally realized I was utterly defeated, and I had lost the wicked game I was playing with crack cocaine. I thought I could always play this game successfully without losing my life. I thought I was invincible, but now I had finally reached my end, and I had lost, and the final price I had to pay was the eternal resting place, or in this case, the eternal un-resting place for my soul in this crack house hell. I was, without a shadow of a doubt, sure that I was in hell and would be separated from God for all eternity. I thought to myself, "How stupid I could have been for allowing this to happen to me when all along I knew better and knew that crack cocaine kills and destroys!" I had always thought, in my arrogance and pride, that this would never happen to me. But now I realized, I had played this game with crack cocaine too many times, and this time the crack finally won. Death had come knocking on my door, and I had answered and let that nasty, grim reaper come on in through the wicked smoke that I was breathing into my lungs. I believed that because I had forsaken my children and abandoned my life to be in this crack house, smoking drugs, it would be my twisted hell forever. I was convinced of this! I was utterly overcome with grief to the point where my soul cracked and shattered into a million pieces, and my spirit agonized over what it had lost forever. I thought that this crack house was my hell, and that this scene of torment would play over and over again for eternity. I was devastated!

This was my reality at that moment! Now, based on this experience on a mental and emotional level, I understand what it must feel like for your soul to fall through the windowpane of life into the fires of hell with no way back. When that room changed, I felt myself shift into a different, alternate reality from the one I had been in. The realm of spiritual wickedness had opened up in that room and swallowed me whole. Although I did not die and hell was not my eternal destination, at that moment, hell became my reality, and I was terrified! At one point, the torment became so unbearable that I finally cried out in anguish—a gut-wrenching, primal scream—and yelled as loud as I could, "Stoooooooooooooopppppp!" That scream was a terror-filled, excruciating cry for help. As you can imagine, it cleared the room of fellow drug addicts, leaving me alone to try to make sense of what was happening. All alone, feeling like I was in the belly of hell, I began to pray. I kept asking God to forgive me, to make this not real, and to get me out of this terrifying, tormenting wasteland. I begged Him to show me that this was not real, crying out to Him to save my soul from hell.

After pleading and begging God for help for some time, I began to feel a calmness move over me, and the room started to change; I could finally breathe again. I slowly came back to my senses and the actual sad reality that I was sitting in a crack house and had abandoned my children and my life, and continuing on this path was seriously leaving my soul and my life in danger. I was under spiritual attack, and once again, the enemy was trying to destroy me through my addiction. Not only was I contending with the enemy of my soul, my addicted flesh, and a mind obsessed with getting high, but I had also become an enemy unto myself by continuing to pour an endless stream of wickedly dangerous drugs into my body with reckless abandon. I knew I was going down fast, and there wasn't anything that could stop my fall. I knew that either prison or death was in my near future. I had been locked up many times before, but now death and hell seemed like the odds-on favorite to be my next destination. This event was the beginning of the end for me, living in the defeat of my addiction, and set me on a crash course encounter with the devil himself and a soul and life-changing deliverance by my Lord and Savior Jesus Christ! My addiction, a modern-day plague, had now come to a final breaking point in the battle for the eternal destination of my soul between the prince of darkness and the Lord of Light, as I was riding the pale horse of death, straight into the darkness and hell of absolute destruction.

II. MY ADDICTION

Mirrors on the ceiling,
The pink champagne on ice
And she said, 'We are all just prisoners here, of our own device'
And in the master's chambers,
They gathered for the feast
They stab it with their steely knives,
But they just can't kill the beast

Last thing I remember,
I was running for the door
I had to find the passage back
To the place I was before
'Relax,' said the night man,
'We are programmed to receive.
You can check out any time you like,
But you can never leave.

~ The Eagles, "Hotel California"

    My addiction, which haunted me for over half my life, was subtly planted in my soul when I started experimenting with forbidden alcohol—something I saw adults drinking and enjoying. At first, like most kids trying to act grown-up, we became curious about how alcohol affected people and wondered why it was so appealing. Everyone was drinking these "spirits," and they all seemed to have a great time. My friends and I began sneaking into our parents' liquor cabinets and garage refrigerators, where this tasty treasure was stored in plenty. We wanted to find out what all the fun was about and how alcohol always seemed to make good times better. We were fascinated and eager to join in. We started cautiously at age fourteen, in eighth grade, by tasting beer, wine, and liquor in small sips—like a gazelle nervously approaching the river for a cool drink on a hot African day, unaware of the danger. Small sips turned into confident drinks, then into bold gulps. By sixteen, as drivers with licenses, we had moved on to more serious drinking—beer, wine coolers, vodka, and whiskey almost every weekend. We became determined to see who could drink the most beer, inventing drinking games or making quick-guzzle beer bongs. We believed that the more we drank, the better—more meant more fun and excitement—so we were all in!

ISAIAH 5:22 (NKJV)
Woe to men mighty at drinking wine, woe to men valiant for mixing intoxicating drink

When I was sixteen, the legal drinking age in Texas was nineteen. With a fake ID, we could easily pass as legal drinkers, and we could now get our hands on our magic potion without taking it from our parents. We thought we had arrived! When fake IDs didn't work, we would cruise the neighborhoods, look for open garages, and practice garage-hopping, where we would run in, open the fridge, and swipe all the promised treasure and liquid gold we could manage. Then, we'd hop into our waiting cars and quickly disappear into the wind with our loot to get our drink on. One way or another, we found ways to get our booze. One day, my friends and I skipped school and went on a neighborhood treasure hunt, driving through back alleys in search of our lost treasure, when we discovered the "X" marks the spot on the treasure map. So, I sent one friend into the garage while I circled my car around the block. We waited for him to come out with the gold, but instead of returning triumphantly with the pirate's bounty, he was stopped by an angry homeowner in the garage, who pointed a shotgun at his face. The homeowner forced my friend to lie on the garage floor until the police arrived. We watched from a distance, but once the cops pulled up, we high-tailed it out of there. The police took my friend in handcuffs to the station, and his mother was called to pick him up. Needless to say, we all got in trouble when he cracked under pressure and fingered us all. Of course, each of us blamed the others, and most of our parents believed us, so no one was in too much trouble—except my friend, who ended up at the police station. We were all on the track team, and when Coach Andrews heard what happened, he made us run laps for days as punishment. At home, we got slaps on the wrist and were told not to do it again. Of course, we listened for a little while and stayed away from garage-hopping, but whenever we were desperate for alcohol, we always fell back into our old wicked ways—uncharted seas of neighborhood piracy! ARRRRGGGGHHH!

During our pursuit of the ultimate buzz and the most exciting parties, we discovered marijuana. Just as we did with alcohol, our good teacher, we started slow and quickly became true "Pot-Heads." Now, we had a collection of tricks that could turn any moment into a party, and we became the ones with the keys to the magic carpet ride that kept the good times rolling! We did all of this mostly unnoticed by our unsuspecting parents, who could never have guessed or imagined what we were up to when they weren't home or when we were away. We operated a rotating traveling circus, pitching our party tent at a friend's house whose parents trusted them to stay home alone while they were out of town for the weekend. There was never a shortage of places to host all the young people eager for our new kind of excitement. This made us quite popular, and we loved being the center of attention and earning the reputation as the "Party" crowd.

Being a teenager caught in the awkward transition between childhood and adulthood, alcohol and marijuana fit like a glove, giving us a glimpse into the adulthood we were quickly being pushed toward, like a runaway freight train. We enjoyed the naughtiness that came with our new companions, alcohol and marijuana, and the rebellion they represented. It made us feel good that our parents couldn't control this part of our lives, and this anarchy against them somehow made us feel in control of a part of ourselves when they controlled every other aspect. Our parents were unaware of what was happening, and it gave us the power to do it behind their backs. Like typical teenagers rocking the boat of the supposed "Good Kid" pleasure cruise, our parents thought they had us on a sailing course toward a bright future—the one they chose for us—and believed it would always be that way.

Being a talented athlete and becoming a well-known football star, in the beginning, I always worked with drinking and pot smoking around the first love in my life, Football! During pre-season training and football seasons, training and performance took priority, and I reined in my partying. I would still partake in the fun and excitement, but football acted as a governor for me, allowing me to stay on top of my game and continue to excel on the gridiron. It was football first, then getting girls, and the party, and then schoolwork, which was always to me just a means by which I could continue to participate in the other three activities.

Alcohol and then marijuana paved the way for other drugs that came later. As a sophomore during spring break, my friends and I rented a beach house on South Padre Island, and I remember a night when some older kids arrived and set our metal toaster on its side, laying out lines of cocaine. I had never seen it before and didn't participate because I was afraid, due to all the negative stories I had heard, along with the "Just Say No" campaign by Nancy Reagan, the First Lady of the early 1980s. I refused to do it and later told my friends clearly, "I will never do cocaine!" By the time we were seniors, not only were we heavily into cocaine, but we also added ecstasy, mushrooms, and methamphetamine, known as "Crank," to our collection of wild fun and excitement. We took ecstasy (MDMA) on weekends and thought nothing of it because, in 1985, it was a legal substance and everyone was using it. It was viewed simply as a supplement that would induce extreme happiness. You could buy it at nightclubs, bars, or even order it from ads in magazines' back pages. At that time in Dallas, Ecstasy was everywhere, and we quickly became heavy users and introduced it to all our friends. I even suspect some of our parents might have been using it, caught up in the craze. Cocaine and meth were different because they were taboo and considered dangerous, but ecstasy had some similar effects. Though taboo among most, cocaine was seen as the "rich man's" drug and had a certain allure because of this label. If you used cocaine, it implied you had money because it was expensive, and as the popular song of the era, White Lines, stated, "Pound for pound it costs more than gold." And believe me, it did. I cannot even come close to estimating how many thousands of dollars I spent on this terrible drug!

I am not sure what happened in just two short years, from age sixteen and "I will never do cocaine!" to my love affair with the substance at eighteen. How on earth did I go from that point of "No-Way" to the point of "Hell-Yes"? That transitional moment when I said "Okay" to cocaine changed my life profoundly, leading me down a path that would plunge me into the heart of the crack cocaine epidemic sweeping through the United States. It was a journey that would consume nearly a quarter of a century of my life. I remember the day I fell in love with cocaine—the night it quickly became my absolute drug of choice because of its incredible rush, euphoric highs, and energizing effects. It was my senior prom night, and my friends and I rented a stretch limo, stocked it with plenty of cocaine for what was supposed to be a memorable night. We stayed at a luxurious hotel downtown where the prom was held. In true 80s fashion, I wore a white tuxedo with tails and a pastel cummerbund made of pink, yellow, and baby blue plaid. It was 1986, and bright colors were all the rage. I felt as cool as I could be. With a big bag of cocaine matching my vivid outfit, I believed I was unstoppable. Throughout the night, before, during, and after the dance, I snorted lines at a dizzying pace, with no intention of stopping. The prom was fun, but the real party was back in the suite—where lines and alcohol flowed endlessly into the early morning. At one point, I was in the bedroom of the suite, sitting on a couch in front of a table piled high with cocaine, snorting line after line without pause. I was like an out-of-control vacuum cleaner, watching the "White Lines" disappear up each nostril. All I wanted was more. I refused to stop as my body was in riot mode, craving the pleasure of each new snort of cocaine, taking me higher and higher into the stratosphere of reckless indulgence.

I was quickly turning into a mess, and my girlfriend at the time—my high school sweetheart who never did drugs—looked at me and asked, "Aren't you going to stop?" I looked up from the pile of cocaine with an arrogant smile and replied, "No." Then I proceeded to snort another line as she yelled, "You are disgusting!" and ran out of the room crying. A few minutes later, realizing I should go find her and bring her back, I left to search for my very upset girlfriend. I ran down the hallway to the elevators and stepped inside. I pressed the down button, and instantly I found myself in a strange, drug-induced alternate reality. As the elevator started moving down, I experienced the most intense euphoric rush I'd ever felt, lifting me to a new high. It felt like I was no longer on this earth, and that time and space had lost all meaning. The elevator continued to descend, but I was soaring upward, higher and higher. The entire elevator was covered with mirrors, and I will never forget that look on my face when I saw myself in one of the mirrors and shouted, "Man, I love this stuff!" Enter the dragon! That was the moment the lie of cocaine became my twisted truth, and my addiction to the seductive, tempting beast of cocaine sank its hooks deep into me, gripping my soul in its destructive trap. I fell for it completely! I believed the dangerous lie that cocaine had magical powers and could be trusted to take me to new heights. I thought I had discovered something extraordinary, mysterious, and dependable for a life filled with fun, excitement, and incredible, mind-blowing euphoria. Surrounded by mirrors reflecting themselves and me as a reflection of that reflection, trapped in a maze of endless euphoria, I thought it would never end. I believed cocaine was a good thing and that I could use it recreationally to take me on more of those wild rides, new trips, and experience a new realm of possibilities.

This was the day I fell in love with cocaine, a day that changed my life forever. I became attached to the mother of all beasts, which was trying to destroy my very soul. All I could see at the time was the good in cocaine, and I was blind to the damage it was causing to my soul and to the harsh reality of the Trojan horse I had just let into my life. That night, I fully accepted cocaine as a gift and let it penetrate deep into my once well-protected city—my soul, which was meant to be God's temple for Him to dwell in. Now, there was a breach, and the enemy used addiction as a weapon, disguising it as a beautiful gift of lady cocaine, gaining a foothold in my inner being that would soon bring down the crumbling walls of my promising life.

The lie of my addiction in the early years appeared to me as a seductive mistress with a beautiful secret to show me—a sweet forbidden truth! I believed I had uncovered some hidden treasure—the holy grail of pleasure. Alcohol and cocaine became my go-to for adventure, entertainment, and escapism. I could always count on them and kept them in my tool belt. They offered me a secret gateway into adulthood and a magical realm, a kind of portal, which opened up a "Pandora's Box" filled with mysterious and enchanting fun and excitement that I could find nowhere else. Alcohol and drugs turned out to be the most magical substances I had ever encountered, giving me an unexpected glimpse into something new and extraordinary. Every time I used them, it was an adventure into the unknown—a journey into a pleasure dome, if you will. The more I indulged, the more incredible experiences I had. It was a treasure chest of fun and excitement, always a trip into the land of adventure.

Cocaine entered my life just as everything was thriving. I was playing college football, and as a true freshman, I made the starting lineup for the Southern Methodist University Mustangs, a team that had been among the best in the nation just a few years earlier. Financially, I didn't have to worry about money. I was well taken care of, traveled the world with my family, drove the nicest sports cars, was becoming a successful football player at the national college level, dated the most beautiful girls, threw and attended the best parties, and always seemed to be the life of the party. I spent money freely, buying drinks and drugs for my friends as we kept the good times rolling! Life felt like one big celebration, with the hope that the good life was here to stay and would never end. I happily jumped aboard the crazy train at full speed, enjoying life in the fast lane and passing through the scenes of my life in a blur, unaware of the massive wall at the end of the line—that was my final destination on this train, which I had unexpectedly chosen, or perhaps it had chosen me. This train was everything to me. The idols of worship I had built up in my life—money, prestige, fame, accolades from sports, arrogance, alcohol, cocaine, self-reliance, and out-of-control pride—were the false gods I worshipped, believing they would bring me happiness and meet all my needs.

On May 5, 1988, in Atlanta, Georgia, I was introduced to crack cocaine for the first time. I was playing football and attending the University of Georgia, where I continued to succeed, just as I had always done on the football field. One of my friends and I drove from Athens to Atlanta to attend a Poison and David Lee Roth concert. Afterward, we decided to find something stronger than alcohol, so we drove around the inner city looking for some "powder" cocaine. As we asked people in different ghettos if they knew where we could find some cocaine, we stumbled upon a man selling crack rock, as they called it. This was something we had only heard about on TV and through news reports, often linked to "The War on Drugs"; this stuff was supposed to be terrible. Terrible, you say? Count me in! We smoked the crack, and it wasn't terrible at all. We thought it was amazing and couldn't wait to try it again. When I left that first crack house early that morning, I handed the guy $40 and thanked him for introducing me to this drug called "Crack." I paid a man to introduce me to something that would ultimately destroy my life. Oh, the irony! Once I smoked my very first crack rock, it took me back to that mirror in the elevator at my high school prom when I first fell in love with cocaine. But this time, it was on a whole new level. If my high school cocaine experience was like a trip to the sky, this Atlanta thing was like attaching myself to a rocket and attempting to break through the firmament! That first time smoking crack planted a desire in me to experience more of this "Terribly Exciting" drug.

Throughout my college years, I balanced a healthy appetite for alcohol and drugs with my studies, holding everything together out of my deep love and passion for football. I would have fallen much earlier into my addiction if it hadn't been for football. I was never willing to lose total control of the drugs because doing so would mean the end of football, and to me, football was my stability in a world that constantly confused me. Football was the only place I felt whole, a refuge where I could escape and vent my anger at a world that was always raging at me. I always played football with fierce yet controlled abandon, which pushed me to the top of the game. Sadly, I later applied that same fierceness to my drug addiction. I went after drugs just like I went after touchdowns on the football field. Looking back at my teenage self, I see a good-looking, kind, compassionate, and happy young man with a future full of promise. I had the potential and a wealth of possibilities to do anything I wanted in this world. I had it all, and I was emerging as a gifted athlete, making a name for myself on the football field, which complemented my family name associated with success. I was well-educated, had many friends, and supportive, loving parents who wanted the best for me and always provided the finest the world could offer. I had great relationships with my two sisters, whom I adored, and my family was positioned for great things as my dad's company took off and became an innovative leader in the telecommunications industry. My dad worked extremely hard and is a highly skilled, intelligent businessman—well-educated with an entrepreneurial spirit. At this point in my life, I was a young man with huge potential and unlimited possibilities, with a bright future almost certainly ahead.

After a successful college football career and being a well-known local sports figure as my team's co-captain, Offensive Most Valuable Player, and All-Conference Receiver, I was drafted into the Canadian Football League. I traveled to Edmonton, Canada, and checked into training camp, ready to embark on the next chapter of my life. I had signed a six-figure contract to play football for two years. My dreams had finally come true, and I became a professional football player. I took great pride in this achievement. Unfortunately, things did not go as planned, and the team cut me after just one week, sending me back home to Dallas, TX, USA. I still had a few classes to complete at the university to earn my bachelor's degree in Economics, so I returned to campus, finished my coursework, and graduated. It was very strange for me to go to school and no longer be a star football player. I was utterly lost. Now, with my degree in hand, I wondered, what's next? So, I ventured into the world of business to make my mark. I grew up with a very successful businessman as my dad, so I decided to follow in his footsteps.

I worked a few sales jobs in the computer hardware and software industry, but nothing ever really clicked for me. It wasn't as exciting as scoring touchdowns, so I lacked passion, which led to average performance. During this time, my alcohol and drug use increased, and I was quickly heading for trouble. I stood at a crossroads: either get serious about my life after football, quit drinking and using drugs, and build a promising future, or continue down the destructive path I was on and face ruin. Do what's right and create a better life, or keep making wrong choices, with no telling where I might end up.

GENESIS 4:7 (NIV)

If you do what is right, will you not be accepted? But if you do not do what is right, sin is crouching at your door; it desires to have you, but you must rule over it."

I made my choice, and soon after, I experienced a great fall. On one hand, I wish I could go back and warn myself about the dangerous allure of alcohol and drugs, and tell that young man that he is about to believe the biggest lie of his life, which will lead him into some of the darkest, deepest places he could ever imagine. I could warn him that it will eventually take everything from him and turn him into a drug addict who commits crimes and ends up in prison. Maybe if I had warned him then, I would not have had to go through the captivity, hell, and darkness of addiction. On the other hand, if I had warned that young man and he had not gotten addicted to drugs, then I would not be the man I am today. I love this man! I also might not have the intimate and close relationship I have today with my Lord and Savior, Jesus Christ. You see, because of my addiction and what I have been through in my life with all my struggles, I have an unbreakable bond with Jesus, who is my best friend. Jesus and I are tight. We are closely intertwined; we are deeply connected to one another. Through the captivity, darkness, and hell of addiction and my deliverance, we have become one. We have wrapped ourselves around each other, and neither one of us is letting go. We are together, and nothing will ever separate us. In conclusion, if I could go back and say anything to that young man, it would be this: "When the going gets tough, and it will, remember this one thing: cry out to Jesus, the savior of your soul!"

ROMANS 8:38-39 (AMP)

For I am convinced [and continue to be convinced—beyond any doubt] that neither death, nor life, nor angels, nor principalities, nor things present and threatening, nor things to come, nor powers, 39 nor height, nor depth, nor any other created thing, will be able to separate us from the [unlimited] love of God, which is in Christ Jesus our Lord.

As a young man, after failing to pursue my dream of becoming a professional football player, I found myself with a wealth of opportunities ahead of me. The sky was the limit, and the world was my oyster. I could go anywhere or do anything I wanted. It's strange to me that I chose the path that led to captivity, darkness, and the hell of addiction, bound by heavy chains. Or did that path choose me? Like a beautiful fish swimming happily in the vast ocean of my life, full of promise and endless juicy worms, I was about to bite into the wrong worm, unaware of the hidden hook of addiction that would unexpectedly take hold of me. I was about to face the fight of my life—a battle that would last most of my adult years and truly be a struggle for my soul and its eternal fate. I did what any unsuspecting fish would do and unknowingly took that bait with a huge bite, only to be caught by the biggest lie of my life! The hook was set, the fight was on, and I was another sucker on the line. I was headed for the boat, then into the frying pan to be cooked and eaten by the mortal enemy of my soul. To say the least, I was in for a world of hurt if I didn't act quickly, and with addiction, nothing is ever quick once you keep fighting. The longer you fight, the more you suffer, and the tougher you must become—or you will be destroyed. At some point, you have to surrender to something greater that can fight for you!

The idea of writing this book came to me while I was in prison, through a revelation—to share my testimony and the gift of poetry I discovered within myself when God opened my eyes to the truth. Everything in life has a rhythm; even in chaos, there is a flow. Even in the captivity, darkness, and hell of addiction, there is a kind of symphony. Poetry is rhythm, just as my addiction was. The ebb and flow—the rhyme and meter—are constant in the battle between spirit and flesh, between light and darkness, between good and evil that make up the ongoing struggle of addiction. I take full responsibility for what happened to me and for what I did to myself and others through my alcohol and drug use. I am the only one at fault for becoming addicted. The first step in overcoming addiction is to accept full responsibility for it. That's why I say "My Addiction," because I own it! And if you own it, then you can overcome it because it's yours to handle as you choose. It's your decision to make. Stop drinking and using drugs, or face death and hell. That is the cold, hard truth! Accept it and choose to live.

My addiction has ruined my life many times over. I could never seem to learn that drinking alcohol and using drugs would eventually lead to destruction. My addiction always took on a life of its own, consuming me and, unfortunately, everyone I loved. It wrapped around me like a snake and refused to let go, and the venom it released was destroying me. My soul's fate was uncertain. Was I going to spend eternity in Heaven with my Lord and Savior Jesus Christ, as

I was taught in Sunday school as a child, or would I burn in hell with those who rejected Him? In my addiction, I was unknowingly at the 'Crossroads,' making a deal with the devil for my soul.

My addiction, once it put its final deadly hook in me, once the snake sank its fangs into my soul and released its hot venom, became an overwhelming, heavy burden of bondage in captivity. I was a slave to my addiction and chained to it as if I were in prison. How can I ever break these chains?

PSALM 107:10 (NKJV)
Some sat in darkness, in utter darkness, prisoners suffering in iron chains

In the beginning, alcohol and drugs were my trusted friends, my companions in a life that always seemed to promise endless adventure and good times. Now they had turned on me and become enemies of my soul. They became weapons wielded by the enemy to drive me into a darkness and hell that looked nothing like the attractive, inviting package I was shown in high school. The alcohol and drugs initially brought fun and excitement—a bag full of good times. Still, very quickly, they turned into a living beast that consumed a quarter-century of my life and led me down some of the most horrible, haunting, and truly evil paths. And now, addiction had begun its destructive work in me, chaining me to itself for a ride into hell itself.

Through my success in football and my dad's example of a strong work ethic, I learned how to work hard, rely on my strengths, and reach my goals. My motto has always been, "Keep Moving Forward." I started trusting my inner resources to achieve my life goals. This self-reliance had never let me down before, and I believed it was the key to success in all areas of life. I believed that when life pushed hard, you should always push back even harder. I was a bulldozer baby! "Go ahead and push me, I like that! Now it's my turn to do the pushing!" That was until I faced my addiction. No matter how hard I tried to defeat this formidable opponent across the line of scrimmage from me, I couldn't seem to win. I became frustrated with my ongoing series of heavy losses. I was scoring zero touchdowns against my addiction. I couldn't find a way to move the ball forward, as it steamrolled over me daily. My own strength failed me when I needed it most, and I started to see myself as weak. But I was determined to prove I was still strong and could beat my addiction if I kept fighting. However, my inability to make progress in this battle damaged my spiraling self-esteem because my identity and self-worth were always deeply rooted in my toughness and ability to overcome obstacles through strength. Once, I was asked the question, "If you were a superhero, what superpower would you possess?" This was easy. I would be like Superman and have superhuman strength so that I could break through anything. In my addiction, the power of my strength was questioned, and I was desperately searching for answers as to why this was happening to me. I had become weak, and to me, that was unacceptable, and I felt ashamed.

As much as I loved the intense high from smoking crack cocaine, I was also addicted to the adrenaline rush that came with the fear of putting myself in dangerous situations. The drugs intensified this by causing paranoia whenever I used them. Many times, when I took a crack hit, I would instantly fear for my life and believe that people were trying to kill me. This put me in a state where every cell in my body, all my senses, and all my thoughts were on high alert, scanning for perceived danger. The massive amounts of adrenaline mixed with the drugs sent me into a war zone. The inner-city ghettos, along with the poverty and suffering I witnessed, were a far cry from the life of privilege and wealth I had known. This was definitely not the "Whitemans" world I had grown up in.

It was fascinating to experience this unfamiliar way of life, which I had never encountered before, and I wanted to learn everything I could about it. I was captivated, confused, intrigued, scared to death, and utterly amazed at this new world I was immersing myself in. I couldn't understand why I had grown up so fortunate with money and opportunity while, at the same time, there were entire communities of people around me who had grown up with nothing, in poverty, violence, crime, and terrible living conditions. I have always found depth, authenticity, and richness in people suffering from poverty, and I was deeply drawn to that. The worse the conditions, the more compelling they were for me. The high from cocaine, the adrenaline from the dangerous surroundings, the intrigue of discovering this new culture, my compassion for those suffering, and my rebellion against a world I had no idea how to fit into created a potent mixture, and I began consuming it in large amounts. I couldn't get enough. It was an alternate reality I could escape into whenever I didn't want to face my current life. The white suburban culture I was born into and had grown bored with couldn't match the excitement and allure of this new world I found in the crack cocaine-filled ghettos.

It was the 1990s, and the crack epidemic of the 1980s was still raging in our inner-city neighborhoods, now spreading into the suburbs and wealthier areas. I eagerly jumped into the chaos with reckless abandon and blind ambition to see what all the fuss was about. The popular song at the time had a lyric that said, "crack killed Apple Jack," but I believed I was no "Apple Jack." I thought I was invincible! I would leave a big, beautiful house in far North Dallas, drive one of the luxury cars we kept in the garage, and head into the inner-city housing projects to get lost for days smoking crack. Later, once I had my own home, those days turned into weeks, and eventually, weeks became months of disappearance. When I answered the call to satisfy the growing addiction inside me, increasing my craving for crack and fear, I blindly raced ahead. I could hear the song in my head from the weekend cartoon, "Go Speed Racer Go!" One thing about me is that I always charge headfirst into chaos and uncertainty at full speed. I did it like I always did on the football field, slamming into oncoming blockers without regard for my body or safety.

Now I was doing the same thing in this strange and wonderfully different culture, and I was captivated. I was all in! The higher the high, the scarier the fear, the wilder the adventure—the more I loved it! It both terrified and thrilled me at the same time. I also began to get a glimpse into a spiritual realm that fascinated me even more, as I experienced the mysterious effects of these dangerous, dark magic street drugs. I couldn't quite explain it, but I always felt that something unseen was lurking nearby, present and watching, and I desperately wanted to understand what it was and why. That forbidden curiosity was a dangerous lure that nearly cost me my life many times, proving the saying true: 'Curiosity killed the cat.'

Soon after I failed to become a professional football player, my life turned into a relentless series of tragic events. On the outside, I seemed to have it all together and was headed for even greater success. Still, I began a series of disappearing acts when I would, in a perfect poetic rhythm, vanish into the dangerous street culture of crack cocaine, leaving no signs of my whereabouts. This pattern became the poetry of my addiction. I appeared to be doing well: I had a good place to live, a nice car, a good sales job, and plenty of money. I would go out and party with friends and usually had a lovely girlfriend. But then, one night, after one too many drinks, I would slip away unnoticed and head to the ghetto, where I knew I'd find my poison.

After several years of my downward spiral and clear evidence of my full-blown addiction to crack cocaine, my family finally decided that enough was enough and sent me to my first drug rehab center. By this point, I had been spending days and weeks in crack houses and wandering the streets with gang members, drug dealers, prostitutes, and other addicts. With my parents' support, I went to rehab, got clean and sober, and managed to stay that way for a while. Usually, after a stint in rehab, I would make some progress in rebuilding my life. This phase typically lasted three to six months, but then I became complacent and overconfident, starting to underestimate how serious my addiction was. I began to believe the false idea that I could drink alcohol normally like everyone else. That first drink would pull me back into the cycle. As predictable as clockwork, I would go to a bar for a few drinks, eventually have one too many, and the crack beast would tap me on the shoulder, demanding to be fed, and I would gladly respond. I'd head out into the night in a drunken haze, easily finding a crack house in a dangerous part of the city, and I'd disappear once again into the land of the living dead. I'd retreat into the dark world of crack cocaine to satisfy the insatiable hunger of my addiction.

It's March 1997, six years after I failed in Canada, and I've just finished another stint in a rehab center, this time in West Palm Beach, Florida. I've relapsed once again. I'm driving around looking for drugs when I see a street dealer and ask him if he has any crack. He said no, but he knew where he could get some. Earlier that day, I broke into a house where I knew a large amount of cash was hidden under a mattress. At my rehab, there was a very wealthy woman and her son detoxing from pain pills and trying to get clean. Once we all got out of rehab, they hosted a party at their house in Palm Beach, and we hung out by their pool. During that day, her son asked me to buy them some alcohol, and I agreed. I saw him go to the bed, lift the mattress, and there was a stash of cash underneath. So now that I am smoking crack again, I know exactly where to go to get money to support my habit. I hit a good "lick" that day, taking $2,000.

So now I am in my car driving a street dealer to an unknown location to get me some crack cocaine to smoke. We pulled up to the housing projects, and I handed him $100 to buy the drugs. I guess he saw all of my stolen cash, because when he came back to the car and I rolled down the window, he stuck a 9mm pistol to my head and told me to give him all my money. With the gun next to my temple, I told him I did not have any more cash. At that point, he cocked the pistol and said, "White boy, you better come off of that cash or I'm going to smoke you!" So, I handed him the money, and he started to walk back into the housing projects. Then I started honking the horn nonstop, and he turned around and approached the car again and stepped up to my window, warning me that he was going to blow my head off if I didn't leave now. That is when I began to bargain with him. I told him that was all the money I had, and I had nowhere to stay that night, and I needed at least $100 for a hotel room. If he would give me back $100, then I would leave. That is when he peeled a $100 bill from the wad of cash he had stolen from me and said,

"Go!" and pointed down the street. I immediately followed those orders and took off into the night, and continued on my way. Then I went right back to the street and bought $100 worth of crack to smoke. This is what I mean when I said I went after drugs just like I went after touchdowns on the football field. Nothing was going to keep me from scoring, not even a pistol to the head.

Before I relapsed, after leaving rehab, I got a job at Home Depot and was renting a room from one of the department managers. Now that I've relapsed and am using drugs again, I've disappeared into the streets, lost my job, and haven't paid my rent. I called my landlord to try to get my belongings, and he told me he'd given all my stuff to Goodwill. He also said that if I tried to come back to his house, he would call the police. I was furious and cussed him out. This became a pattern for me. I would get my life together with a car, a job, and a place to live, thinking this time would be different. Then, once everything was in order, I'd take a drink, which would lead to crack, and then I was off to the races once again, leaving a trail of wreckage behind.

That is when I decided to get into my car and drive to Key West to pick up a stripper I had met a few weeks earlier. We planned to drive up to New Jersey, where she's from, and smoke drugs the whole way. When I arrived in Miami around midnight, I pulled over and called my mom to share my plans with her. She asked me what in the hell I was thinking, and I replied, "Mom, I am sick and tired of getting high, but I can't stop getting high. Goodbye." Leaving Miami on Highway 1, heading into the Florida Keys in my Infiniti Q45, I became angry and felt as though I no longer wanted to live. I began drinking the alcohol I had stolen from a grocery store earlier that day, and was smoking the last of my crack. The alcohol started to kick in, and I became distraught and felt like I did not want to live anymore. I got the crazy idea to take my car full speed over the crest of the 7-Mile Bridge and jump it into the ocean below. I was pissed off, suicidal, high on alcohol and cocaine, and I screamed at God out of the sunroof of my car at the top of my lungs, "God, you made me like this. It is your fault that I am this way!" At one point during this meltdown, I drove past a Highway Patrolman at 136 MPH in a 45 MPH zone. Once I did that, the chase was on, and I wasn't going to stop at any cost. I was all in and headed for the 7-Mile Bridge, and my destiny with death, or so I thought. God had other plans for me that night, other than jumping my car off the 7-Mile Bridge. Just before I reached the bridge, the police set up a roadblock with stinger spikes that would flatten my tires. I did not make it to the bridge, and I was arrested. The Miami Herald newspaper reported the incident the next day on the front page of the Florida Keys section.

MIAMI HERALD, THE (FL) - MARCH 22, 1997
DEPUTIES USE SPIKES TO STOP FLEEING CAR ON U.S. 1 DRIVER REACHED TOP SPEED OF 136 MPH

Author: Herald Keys Bureau
Metal spikes stopped a motorist driving erratically down U.S. 1 at speeds up to 136 mph early Friday. Charles Michael Bowen, 29, of Palm Beach Gardens, refused to stop his car for Monroe deputies at mile marker 89. At that time, he was traveling 71 mph in a 45-mph zone, deputies said. Bowen was also seen passing in no-passing zones and turn lanes, said Deputy Becky Herrin, sheriff's spokeswoman. Deputies radioed colleagues down the road, telling them to look out for the 1997 Infiniti, Herrin said. Deputies deployed stinger spikes - metal spikes embedded in a rubber strip that puncture small holes in tires, causing the car to stop without harming the driver - to stop Bowen at U.S. 1 and Coco Plum Road in Marathon. He was charged with fleeing and eluding police, driving under the influence of alcohol, possession of cocaine and drug paraphernalia, and reckless driving. In the Infiniti were beer and wine bottles and a pipe with crack cocaine residue, Herrin said.

Copyright (C) 1997 The Miami Herald
Record Number: 9703240151

I was arrested that night and taken to Monroe County Jail. I spent the first three days alone in a cell on suicide watch, and afterwards, I was moved to the general population. When I entered the main dorm, everyone started calling me "Speed-Racer" because they saw my story in the newspaper. That nickname stuck with me for the rest of my time there. I spent another two weeks in jail before being transferred to a treatment center in Miami. When my court date arrived, I only received probation, with no additional jail or prison time. During my sentencing, when the judge spoke, she said, "Mr. Bowen, let it be known that you are getting a gift from Monroe County today on your charges." When my parents learned I was in jail, my dad flew to the Florida Keys, hired the judge's divorce attorney with a substantial amount of money, and somehow convinced the judge to be lenient. Once again, I bought into the lie that I could drink alcohol and act normal, believing I could control my addiction. But as soon as I took that first hit of crack cocaine, anything could happen—and usually did.

In the spiritual realm, the devil's main tactic, which controls his weapon of addiction, is to plant ideas, thoughts, and suggestions into our minds. He then deceives us into thinking they are our own by mimicking our inner voice, causing us to obey and follow them. This is the insanity of my addiction, where everything screams so loudly that I cannot drink alcohol normally because every time I do, I end up smoking crack and destroying my life. My flesh screams for pleasure, and my mind convinces me that this time will be different, while the pride inside me puffs up with the need to prove myself. I have been a failure and have repeatedly shown that I am unable to drink alcohol and use drugs recreationally like people who do it and don't become addicted. I always feel like I must prove I can be normal, too. I become prideful and believe I am strong and in control when, in reality, I am not. The voice in my head tells me that this time will be different—that I won't fall apart. And I believe it!

My attitude comes from childhood experiences playing football and other sports, which shaped a mindset of always feeling like I had something to prove. Alcohol and drugs wouldn't control me; I would fight them and prove I could overcome them. I was challenged, confused, and furious, and whenever I faced these situations, I did what football had taught me. I would hunker down, face the fight, confront the challenge head-on, and run fearlessly into it, crashing headfirst, hoping to come out on top—just like covering kick-offs on the football field. That was just my nature, and I approached every challenge in my life that way. Unfortunately, this is the worst way to deal with the tricky, powerful weapon of addiction. The devil uses pride and our ego against us. He pokes and prods us like cattle, pushing us closer to falling into the trap of addiction. He plants thoughts, ideas, and suggestions that belittle us and make us feel bad about ourselves by telling us we are weak and failures because we can't control something as simple as alcohol and drugs. Then he shows us others who are successful and makes us believe that we too can be like them if we try again.

We listen to the devil and his lies. He preys on our competitiveness, our desire to be winners, and our need for control. He encourages us by telling us we are strong enough and smart enough to handle things on our own. At the same time, he mimics our inner voice because he knows we are more likely to trust ourselves—our arrogance and self-confidence—rather than an unfamiliar voice. He speaks to us in our minds, pretending to be the voice of truth, planting new thoughts or bright ideas about how we can control our addiction and enjoy the full benefits of drinking alcohol and using drugs without negative consequences. In this internal dialogue, we believe we are talking to ourselves, but he persuades us that we can beat our addiction and return to normal. Once we accept this lie and rebel against the truth, we relapse into drinking and drug use, losing control just as we always do, and the devil gains another captive. Now, we are once again ensnared, chained to our fleshly desires through alcohol and drugs. Repeatedly turning to alcohol and drugs to satisfy our fleshly desires is a sign of rebellion against the truth, which is considered witchcraft. We find ourselves in bondage to sin—precisely where the enemy has led us.

1 SAMUEL 15:23 (NKJV)

For rebellion is as the sin of witchcraft, and stubbornness is as iniquity and idolatry. Because you have rejected the word of the LORD, he also has rejected you from being king."

When we invite sin into our lives, we open the door for the devil to control our minds. Once he takes control, he can lead us to commit all kinds of sins through our actions. In the physical world, this can manifest as alcoholism, drug addiction, breaking the law, and becoming a criminal, as in my case. Society often views us as bad people because we lie, cheat, steal, break promises, and lose our moral compass—doing things we never thought we would do. As a result, we often end up in jail, prison, rehab centers, hospitals, or even lose our lives. Spiritually, we become servants of sin, turning alcohol and drugs into idols, worshiping them, and unknowingly serving the devil. The devil, being the god of this world, seeks his own children to worship him, and when we fall into addiction, we fall into his trap, and we are doing just that. We worship the devil when we serve the worthless idols he puts in front of us. Addiction blinds us to the truth and takes control of our lives. We become chained to addiction and bound to death by our sins.

EPHESIANS 4:4 (NIV)

The god of this age has blinded the minds of unbelievers, so that they cannot see the light of the gospel that displays the glory of Christ, who is the image of God.

In this realm of devil and idol worship, we find ourselves entangled in all kinds of sin. Once we are bound by our sins, like prisoners in chains, it becomes impossible to escape. We get trapped, lose hope, become discouraged, and start experiencing all sorts of emotional stress and pain. Our only option is to turn to the one thing we can't escape—our addiction to alcohol and drugs that dominates us. We seek comfort in the very things that cause all the problems in the first place. This creates the vicious cycle of addiction. Round and round we go, where we stop, only the good Lord knows.

In my case, I would act as my own cheerleader, encouraging myself and convincing myself that I would not fall back into the same cycle as before. These lies that this time would be different came from the devil himself, whispering in my mind. I believed them because I genuinely wanted to be like other people—able to control alcohol and drugs and use them recreationally. I accepted these lies as truth because my inner voice was the one telling me, so of course, I believed them. My downfall was trusting myself and always thinking I knew better than anyone else what was good for me. People could tell me straight to my face that I was an alcoholic and drug addict who couldn't control his use, and I would refuse to believe it, even though years of evidence proved otherwise. Time and again, I tried to drink socially and control it like normal people, but every single time, I ended up on a full-blown crack cocaine binge into the unknown. One day, I seemed to have everything together, moving forward on the right track, and then, in an instant, I was gone—off to the races once again. My life was run by self-will run riot! I would get so caught up in the idea of recapturing the early years of recreational drinking and drug use, believing I could somehow find the right balance to unlock that hidden part of myself and go back to how things used to be. But that never happened.

I would motivate myself and talk myself into giving it another try, then rush out to test my new idea of becoming a recreational drinker and drug user again. Sometimes I could manage some decent control during the first few attempts out in the field. Still, eventually, I would take that one fatal drink, and the door would swing wide open, allowing my addiction to rush in and take over, pulling me back into the deep, dark corners of a crack cocaine nightmare. I might be drinking "responsibly" one moment, then suddenly, it's like the phone ringing or a tap on my shoulder—if I answered or looked back, it was over. Suddenly, I'd shift gears, and the speeding car of addiction would be back on the road again, unknowingly heading down a destructive path on another drug binge, disappearing into the unknown, leaving my life and responsibilities behind. At some point, I'd find myself staring down another crack pipe, gazing into a wickedly flickering flame in the smoke-filled room of a shady, broken-down crack house, hiding from the harsh reality of my life. This was the moment I always dreaded—when I realized I had lost control and wouldn't be coming out anytime soon. The waves of disappointment, guilt, shame, fear, and terror gripped me tightly and refused to let go. These feelings fueled the fire that kept me locked in a struggle against myself and my failing sanity. Crying inside, my spirit was shouting to be free. Meanwhile, my mind kept telling me to smoke more drugs. In this chaotic storm, my body responded by acting out my craving to get drunk and high, and through this process, the darkness of addiction began its destructive work within me.

After I left the rehabilitation center in Miami, I persuaded my parents to pay for an apartment in South Beach. It turned out to be a disastrous decision. South Beach in Miami is one of the last places on earth where a recovering alcoholic and crack cocaine addict should live. But once again, my pride got in the way, and I thought I could handle it. This wasn't just any apartment; it was a studio in the Shelborne Hotel, with a window overlooking the pool and the beautiful white sands of South Beach, Miami. It was party time 24/7, all year long. I lasted exactly one week before I relapsed, sitting by the pool, ordering a cocktail. That cocktail led to another, then another, and by night's end, I was out on the streets looking for something stronger. I found it two blocks away and started smoking crack again. I spent the next four months wandering the streets and beaches, shoplifting, and writing bad checks to keep myself drunk and high.

After four months of this insanity, I finally gave up and told my parents to get me the hell out of Florida. They agreed, so I packed my belongings and flew to Colorado, moving to Vail in the Rocky Mountains, hoping not to catch that Rocky Mountain High vibe you hear in John Denver's song of the same name. This time, in the mountains, I managed to stay away from crack cocaine, mainly because there wasn't any there, but I drank heavily, smoked pot, and ate psychedelic mushrooms often. So, I did live out the words of that song, just in a different way from my usual crack cocaine adventures in the ghetto! There aren't any ghettos in Vail, Colorado. You'd have to go to Denver for those. So, what do you think I ended up doing?

After spending about nine months living in the mountains, I decided it was a good idea to move to Denver and attend real estate school to get my license. However, that didn't work out because I was drawn to the ghetto, where crack cocaine was flowing like water. Like a fish, I jumped into an ocean full of sharks. The cycle just kept going. This time, I found myself running around in the Five Points projects just north of downtown. I had been introduced to one of the street gangs there when I visited their trap houses and smoked crack. For some reason, they liked me and always let me come inside and smoke. I would drive them around to sell drugs and let them use my car, so they kept me close and protected. Sometimes, I would go out and write bad checks, then buy groceries and other items for their families. I also got involved in a more serious hustle by purchasing weapons from gun stores and trading them to gang members for fist-sized rocks of crack cocaine. I remember buying AK-47s, MAC-10 machine pistols, and some 9mm's. I'm not sure what I was thinking at the time, but I was definitely out of my mind and out of control.

One time, I was driving a car full of gangbangers in the hood, and the Denver Police pulled us over, and when they came to my window and saw who was all in the car, they asked me to step out of the vehicle. They walked me to the back of the car and asked if I was okay and if I was in any danger. I told them no, that I was fine. Then they said to me, all serious, "Do you know who you have in the car with you?' I responded, 'Yes, these are my friends; we have been knowing each other for a long time.' Of course, that was a lie. They looked at me funny and told me to get back in the car. They ran all of our names in their system, and we came back clean, so they had to let us go.

During that same period, I was in another crack house within the same projects, smoking, and I had smoked way too much. I started having seizures on the kitchen floor. The people inside the house panicked, took my keys out of my pocket, threw me into the front yard, and drove off in my car. I was left in the yard, flopping around like a fish out of water during a full-blown cocaine overdose. The only thing that saved my life that night was a woman in the house, who called 911, sat with me in the yard, and held my head in her lap until help arrived. I remember regaining consciousness in the back of the ambulance, trying to fight and cursing at the EMTs because I didn't understand what had happened to me. I went to the emergency room until I was stable. They pumped me full of medicine to lower my heart rate so I would stop having seizures. They were afraid I was going to have a stroke. You might think that would be enough to make me quit smoking, but as soon as I was released from the hospital, I went straight back to the crack house and started smoking again. I had no idea where my car was, so I reported it stolen. I learned that in the drug game, you can get your vehicle back faster if you report it stolen. Sure enough, the people driving the car were pulled over, arrested, and taken to jail. When the police contacted me, I told them I didn't want to press charges, which resulted in their release from jail. That earned me a little street cred once the word spread in the hood that the white boy was looking out for the homies!

After about five months on this crazy adventure, I finally left the projects. I moved into a sober living home, where I worked for the program director's business installing tubular skylights in homes around Denver and Colorado Springs. He let me use one of his company trucks for work. My sobriety this time lasted only about three months. I found myself caught up in another bad drinking experiment. After a decade of constant relapses on crack cocaine, visits to around twelve different treatment centers, and numerous incarcerations, my path over the last eight years—following my failure in professional football—took me from Texas to Florida and now to Colorado. I believed each new place would give me a different outcome, but it never did. The idea that a geographical cure works is a myth because wherever you go, you are there, and your addiction follows. One Friday after work, with my paycheck in hand, I headed out for a few drinks. This time, the phone rang after just the second drink, and I answered the call for some crack. Ring, ring, hello—I was heading back to the Five Points projects and knew where to go. After driving around for a while, I met a woman who told me she knew where we could go to smoke. We went into a rowhouse in the projects, and I found what I had been searching for. I placed a crack rock on the pipe, fired it up, and settled in for yet another escape into the realm of the living dead.

On about the sixth day in the crack house, with no food, no sleep, and massive amounts of crack, I came out of a daze. Sitting across from me was a guy nicknamed "Egg-Man" because he sold eggs and crack in the projects. He was shirtless, sitting at a table, cutting rocks from a larger piece of crack cocaine. As he did this, my spiritual eyes opened, and I saw the devil coming through him—his skin was as red as a tomato. When he slid three crack rocks across the table to me, they looked like demon heads, moving and mocking me, revealing their presence. I was shocked, trying to make sense of what I was seeing. I had somehow entered the supernatural, which was both terrifying and captivating. I was completely freaked out and went into a state of high alert. My fight-or-flight response kicked in. I had somehow opened a portal into the realm of spiritual wickedness and was able to see what was happening in the spirit world while the people in the room were using drugs.

After a while, my vision returned to normal, and I started to think the people in the room were trying to harm me. A voice kept telling me they were trying to slip me knockout drugs that would make me pass out so they could do terrible things to me. Every instinct told me to get out of there immediately, but the crack had me trapped. I was chained to the crack house. My mind was screaming to run, preferring flight over fight, but my addiction wouldn't let me leave. Finally, I managed to pull myself away from the crack and left the house, determined never to come back. As I drove away, the craving for rock immediately called me back to that crack house. I was caught in a struggle—my instincts warned me I was in danger, that the people inside wanted to hurt me, but my addiction told me to go back for more. I was torn between the two. I was in a serious battle! In the end, my addiction won, and I returned to the crack house, but before going back, I stopped at a store and bought a steak knife for protection. With a knife in my pocket, I thought that if anything bad happened, I could defend myself with the knife. What I did not realize is that a murderous spirit was attempting to take control of my mind.

    I went back into the house and began smoking crack again with the steak knife in my pocket. After a few puffs off the crack pipe, the devil started whispering to me that these men were going to slip me drugs, knock me out, and rape me. That is when I put my hand in my pocket, gripped the handle of the steak knife, and began looking at the men in the room and figuring out where I was going to stab them if they came my way. I had decided I would stab them in the neck if they made any sudden moves. The thoughts in my mind kept trying to get me to act and stab these people before they could hurt me. I began to hear voices in my head telling me that the men in the room were going to hurt me and that I should stab them now! The voice screamed, "Do it, do it!" This was one of the most intense inner struggles I have ever had to deal with in my life. It took everything that I could muster not to pull out my knife and stab these people in the neck. I came within seconds of committing a triple homicide that day! It was that close. Thank you, Jesus. As I look back at this incident, I realize the enemy was using my addiction against me to try to destroy me and others and have me murder these people. We know the devil only comes to kill, steal, and destroy, and this day he was there to do all three.

JOHN 10:10 (NKJV)

The thief does not come except to steal, and to kill, and to destroy. I have come that they may have life, and that they may have it more abundantly.

This is the horror and terror that comes with the crack cocaine nightmare. The chemicals in the drugs, combined with a lack of food, the dark magic properties of the drugs, and the manipulation from the enemy in the mind, all work together like a witch's brew to bring about our destruction. When you ingest these drugs and do not eat food, you are fasting to spiritual wickedness. The wickedness is in the drugs and acts as a key to open a spiritual portal in the mind that the enemy and his demonic forces use to invade our souls, wreak havoc on our spirits, and drive the drug user to do unspeakable acts, including acts of violence and murder. When you smoke drugs, you bring evil spirits into your body through the smoke. I have experienced this myself, firsthand, on many occasions. The devil tempts us with our desire for the pleasure we believe the drugs will bring us. Through these desires, we are enticed into using drugs, which leads us deeper into our addiction. And the root of all drug addiction is sin. If you do not address the root, then you will never solve the problem of drug addiction.

JAMES 1:14-15 (NKJV)

But each one is tempted when he is drawn away by his own desires and enticed. Then, when desire has conceived, it gives birth to sin; and sin, when it is full-grown, brings forth death.

There is a reason the devil is called the prince of the power of the air, and nothing demonstrates this more than in a crack house, where smoke hangs thick in the air and that air fills your lungs. The devil reveals his wickedness through the smoke, and unclean spirits under his control use it to open our souls and possess our bodies. By inhaling the smoke in rebellion against God, we give the demonic realm legal access to our bodies. Drug use is an abomination to God and deserves His wrath. When we smoke drugs, we invite unclean spirits to dwell in our temples made of clay. By this very nature, we are children of disobedience, children of wrath. We need a Savior!

EPHESIANS 2:1-3 (NKJV)

As for you, you were dead in your transgressions and sins, in which you once walked according to the course of this world, according to the prince of the power of the air, the spirit who now works in the sons of disobedience, among whom also we all once conducted ourselves in the lusts of our flesh, fulfilling the desires of the flesh and the mind, and were by nature children of wrath, just as the others.

Spiritual hosts of wickedness try to influence the physical world, and it seems easier for them to do so if they inhabit a physical body. We see this in the scriptures when Jesus casts out the demons from the man who lives in the tombs of the graveyard and allows them to enter the pigs. Unclean spirits or demons desire a body to make their home. They want to be an indwelling spirit, to be like God and His Holy Spirit. And so does the devil. I believe the devil uses unclean spirits that possess us through drugs to prepare us for a future time when he will ask us to let him come into our souls to dwell. As you will read later in this book, I had this encounter.

MARK 5:11-13 (AMP)

Now there was a large herd of pigs grazing there on the mountain. And the demons begged Him, saying, "Send us to the pigs so that we may go into them!" Jesus gave them permission. And the unclean spirits came out [of the man] and entered the pigs.

This is what I saw when the "Egg-Man" slid the three crack rocks across the table to me. I saw the spiritual key in the crack cocaine rocks that allows unclean spirits to possess the people who smoke those drugs. I believe God let me see what was happening in the spiritual realm as we smoked drugs so that I could understand the spiritual side of drug use, and one day I could warn others, like I am doing here. I wrote the poem "SEEDS," which you can read at the end of this chapter, that illustrates this understanding.

MATTHEW 12:43-45

"When an unclean spirit goes out of a man, he goes through dry places, seeking rest, and finds none. Then he says, 'I will return to my house from which I came.' And when he comes, he finds it empty, swept, and put in order. Then he goes and takes with him seven other spirits more wicked than himself, and they enter and dwell there; and the last state of that man is worse than the first. So shall it also be with this wicked generation."

Do you now understand that your body was not made to contain this evil, dark-magic smoke filled with wickedness? We are playing a dangerous game by smoking drugs and inviting unclean spirits into vessels meant to be filled with God's Holy Spirit. Our bodies, created from the dust of the earth, are not meant to be inhabited by spiritual hosts of wickedness in heavenly places. Your body is a temple, reserved to be filled with the Holy Spirit when you surrender your life to Jesus Christ, believe in His name, and are born again. This is when you are born of the Spirit and become a child of God. The devil is trying to take this from you and replace it with his dark forces—only a cheap imitation of what God has prepared for His children. The devil seeks to steal you from God and trap you in a drug-smokehouse or any form of drug addiction so you will die in your sins and go to hell.

1 CORINTHIANS 6:19 (NIV)

Do you not know that your bodies are temples of the Holy Spirit, who is in you, whom you have received from God? You are not your own;

The next morning marked the seventh day without food or sleep. For six long days, I faced some of the most intense spiritual evil I had ever encountered in my years of drug use. After a difficult night battling paranoia and trying to understand what I had seen in the spiritual realm, I found myself at another house across a field from the projects. The "Egg-Man," who had looked like the devil the night before, was there, along with the woman who owned the house. She had cooked everyone some food because it was Good Friday, two days before Easter Sunday. After the meal, I went into another room with the woman who saved my life when I overdosed in the crack house, and they threw me out into the yard. She and I sat on a futon and started talking about how we believed the "Egg-Man" was giving us both knockout drugs and trying to harm us.

As we sat on the futon, I looked up at the drop ceiling in the middle of the room, and there was a picture of Jesus. Below the image of Jesus was a red chair placed right in the center of the room. What follows next is one of the most incredible spiritual awakenings I have ever experienced in my life. I hope you all are ready for this! While I discussed what I thought was happening at the "Egg-Man's" house with the woman, I started to feel a presence entering the room. For some reason, I kept telling her that the room was filling with angels. I asked her, "Can't you see them?" This was strange because I couldn't see them myself, but something inside me was screaming that angels were flooding into the room. It was as if they were pouring in like water over a waterfall, from the ceiling down over the walls. That's the best way I can describe it. As this continued, my confidence grew, and I became furious at the "Egg-Man." Just as I was about to go into the other room to confront him, he walked into ours and sat down in the red chair under the picture of Jesus facing us. It was "Go-Time".

I rose to my feet and moved toward him; as I did, the entire room seemed to transform and open up. I found myself in a spiritual vision. The room had become a vast valley, with the "Egg-Man" sitting in the middle at the lowest point. I later named this valley the Valley of Decision after reading the book of Joel, Chapter 3, in my Bible. In this vision, I was standing on a hill, facing forward and slightly to my right, with the hill sloping downward toward the valley floor. When I looked to my right, following the slope downward, I saw countless angels in full armor, shimmering with a mix of polished metal and light, their shining brightness illuminating the scene. It felt like battalions of angels were on that hill, all facing the "Egg-Man," who was seated in a red chair on the valley floor. The sky above was completely dark, yet the angels' armor radiated a luminous glow. Then I looked to my left, upward to the ridge above, where I saw the silhouette of a man in a purple robe, gazing into the valley below from the highest point on that hill, standing still as if to say, 'Go ahead, proceed.' The Lord is a man of war: the Lord is his name— Jesus Christ: King of kings.

2 KINGS 6:16-17 (NKJV)

So, he answered, "Do not fear, for those who are with us are more than those who are with them." And Elisha prayed, and said, "lord, I pray, open his eyes that he may see." Then the LORD opened the eyes of the young man, and he saw. And behold, the mountain was full of horses and chariots of fire all around Elisha.

After glancing down to my right and then to my left, I moved toward the "Egg-Man" and stood just inches from his face. I loomed over him as he sat in the red chair, shouting and demanding answers about the knockout drug. He began to stammer and stutter, and I yelled even louder, feeling a rush of incredible power. Suddenly, I saw a demon emerge from him. As this happened, the scene shifted— the valley disappeared, and the room reappeared. Yet, I could still see the demon trying to escape. At that moment, the demon ran up the wall toward the ceiling. When it reached the junction of the wall and ceiling, it vanished through the cornice. The demon was four-legged, brown, slimy, with a thick body and a large, thick tail ending in a triangular tip, giving it a pointed appearance.

Once the demon left him and escaped from the room, the "Egg-Man" panicked and rushed to the front door of the house, trying to get out. Somehow, when he reached the door, I was already there to meet him. At the door, we shared one last exchange, and I looked into his eyes, which resembled the lens of an old handheld extendable telescope—one you might see a pirate looking through. The last thing I noticed was his eyes rolling back as the telescope was being closed and pushed down, then his eyes returned to normal. At that moment, I became aware of my surroundings, and the room went silent. The other people in the house, after witnessing what had happened, ran out as the "Egg-Man" hurried across the field that separated the house from the projects where his apartment was located.

After all this, I walked back into the room and spoke to the woman who stayed with me during my overdose, asking her if she had seen the angels too. She looked at me with a wonderstruck gaze and said, "That wasn't your voice coming out of you!" She told me she saw everything. I believe the enemy uses the chemicals in drugs and their ability to make us fast and not sleep to work within us, bringing about spiritually wicked visions and revealing himself to those caught in his trap. I believe that the enemy was up to his old tricks the night before, and Jesus had seen enough. He came to my rescue, showing me His incredible power and giving me this understanding so I could share it with you, the readers of this book. I believe the devil that day fell into his own trap, which he had set for me. King Jesus is sovereign. King Jesus can swat the devil like you would swat a pesky fly buzzing around your head. Jesus will never leave us nor forsake us, and He will always protect us as His own. Jesus is not bound by time, and I have always been His evangelist, even back in 1999 in a crack house in the ghettos of Denver, Colorado, smoking drugs and chained to sin and darkness. He created me for a purpose, and He will always fight for me so I can fulfill that purpose to the glory of the Father. The devil wanted me dead that day, but God said, "No, my son will live." You can draw your own conclusion about what you think happened to me in that room. Whether you believe it was just a drug-induced hallucination or a spiritual vision from God is up to you. I am writing to provide you with the details of what happened to the best of my ability, by the revelation of the Holy Spirit.

After I finished talking to my friend, we decided to leave the ghetto and drove away in my boss's truck, heading straight to the First United Methodist Church downtown. To give you an idea of where we went, I will describe this church. It was built in 1859 using gray, pink, and purple-colored rhyolite lava rock and purple-colored Utah sandstone. The steeple towers more than 181 feet tall and is topped with a giant bronze cross. There are gargoyles on all sides of the building, which are grotesque figures intended to ward off evil spirits. The belief is that these figures protect the church and its congregation. There are also beautiful, large stained-glass windows throughout, and the altar is magnificent. There is also a massive pipe organ, said to be priceless, which spans an entire wall in the sanctuary. At the time, I had no idea why I was going there, but once I arrived, I knew I had been led there by God.

I lay on the altar in the sanctuary and began to weep, asking God to forgive me. I stayed there until I finally found peace within myself, then I left, knowing something very significant had just happened to me. On my way out of the church, I stopped by the office and told the three ladies there that I was just in a valley full of angels with Jesus Christ and saw a demon leave a man's body. You can imagine their response. God bless their souls; they weren't ready for me. They referred me to a homeless shelter and said they could help me with my drug problem. Coming down from an incredible high after this unbelievable event, I decided to drive back to the projects, park, and get some rest. I pulled over because I was exhausted from the experience and the lack of sleep, and I was no longer using the crack cocaine that usually kept me awake. I fell asleep. When I woke up, my friend was gone, and I realized I should get back to the sober house and ask them to take me back in after my relapse. I was driving downtown just before sunset. It was April 2, 1999, which happened to be Good Friday, a day I believe is perfect for entering what I call the Valley of Decision, described in Joel Chapter 3, also known as the Valley of Jehoshaphat. I wrote a poem about this experience, titled "THE VALLEY OF DECISION," that you can read at the end of this chapter.

JOEL 3:9-14 (NKJV)

"Prepare for war! Wake up the mighty men, let all the men of war draw near, let them come up. Beat your plowshares into swords and your pruning hooks into spears; let the weak say, 'I am strong.'" Assemble and come, all your nations, and gather together all around. Cause Your mighty ones to go down there, O Lord. "Let the nations be wakened, and come up to the Valley of Jehoshaphat; for there I will sit to judge all the surrounding nations. Put in the sickle, for the harvest is ripe. Come, go down; for the winepress is full, the vats overflow - for their wickedness is great." Multitudes, multitudes in the valley of decision! For the day of the Lord is near in the valley of decision.

Still very tired, and now driving through downtown, leaving the projects, I decided to pull over again and lie down because I felt like I was about to pass out, and I did not want to wreck the truck. I pulled over to the side of the street, stopped the truck, and immediately lay down in the front seat. What I did not realize was that I had just run two red lights, and the police were behind me. Needless to say, I did not wake up when they commanded me out of the vehicle, and by the time I finally woke up, they had both sides of the street blocked off and were pulling me out at gunpoint. I went to jail, was charged with driving under the influence, booked, and then taken into a room and questioned by two police officers. They had given me a blood alcohol test, and I had zero alcohol in my blood. They started running me through tests, trying to figure out what kind of drugs I was on. One of the police officers said to the other officer, "I know he is on something. Did you see his eyes when we pulled him from the vehicle?" That always stuck with me. Maybe it wasn't the drugs in my eyes they saw, perhaps it was something else? Then they turned off the lights in the room and started shining a little flashlight in my eyes, and when they could not figure out the drugs I was on, they put in their reports that I was on marijuana. This is strange because I had not smoked any marijuana for almost a year, so it wasn't marijuana. Nevertheless, that was what I was charged with. Driving under the influence of marijuana. That is funny considering everything that happened leading up to my arrest.

After my tests, I was taken to the drunk tank with others under the influence of alcohol and drugs. I found a bed and lay down for the night. About three hours later, to my surprise, I was released around 2:00 a.m. It was early Saturday morning, and I was completely out of money, but I flagged down a cab outside the jail anyway. When I got in, I made a deal with the driver: I would give him my Liberty Bowl Championship Watch in exchange for a ride to my sober house. Once there, I sneaked inside and went down to the basement where my room was located. I got into bed and fell asleep. Around 5:00 a.m., I woke up to find two Denver Police officers re-arresting me because they said they had made a mistake and had accidentally released me when I was supposed to stay in jail. They put me in the back of their police car, took me downtown, where I was rebooked, and placed me in a cell.

I slept all day and night Saturday and finally woke up Sunday morning around 9:00 a.m., which was Easter Sunday, to the call for church. We had a service in the day room, and I will never forget the Pentecostal preacher who delivered the Word that morning. He was old and frail, wearing a brown suit with a coffee-stained shirt and an outdated tie. The one thing I will never forget is his piercing blue eyes, and he spoke with passion and conviction, like fire. After his sermon, I asked him to pray over me, and he laid his hands on me, prayed, and then left. As soon as he left, they called out my name and told me they were releasing me due to overcrowding. This was an odd sequence of events and an Easter weekend I will never forget in full detail. I know for sure that God had His hands on me, and I was in that jail so that the preacher could pray over me.

Once I was released from jail, I contacted my parents and told them everything that happened, including seeing Jesus and the angels. They thought I had lost my mind and immediately told me I needed help. The next day, they flew me to Tucson, AZ, and placed me in another treatment center called Sierra Tucson, which was one of the best in the country. This place resembled a resort, an oasis at the foot of the Catalina Mountains in the Sonoran Desert. I call this place my "Rock-n-Roll" Rehab because I was there with a famous rock star, and we became friends during our treatment. The desert is beautiful to me, and the smell after a good rain is one of my favorite scents in the world. At that time, my parents owned a home on the Westin La Paloma Golf Course, so once my three months of rehab were over, I moved in with them and decided to make Tucson, AZ, my new home. I was clean and sober, and I believed I would never drink or do drugs again. Initially, I did.

I lived with my parents for about six months and started attending 12-step recovery meetings, church, and engaging in activities that supported my sobriety. I believed I had built a strong foundation in recovery and decided it was time to get my own place. I moved into an apartment near my parents' house in the Catalina Mountain Foothills and got a job as a sales representative with WorldCom. I met a woman, we started dating, and I got her pregnant. I thought this would be the one thing to keep me clean and sober—becoming a father for the first time. Boy, was I wrong. Once again, I started drinking, and my life began to fall apart—only now, the stakes were much higher, and I had more to lose. I began drinking almost daily after work, then I started snorting cocaine when I met a customer who turned out to be a cocaine dealer. I could drink and snort cocaine with some control and not lose it completely. I did this for several months. During this brief period, I believed I could handle recreational use of both.

With newfound confidence, I decided to take a trip to Las Vegas to meet my best friend, Ryan Fishman, and his new girlfriend, Genie, whom he had fallen in love with. They would eventually marry and have children. They stayed in a suite at the Rio Hotel and Casino because they were both in the fashion industry and attending a trade show. Ryan knew I was drinking but didn't know I was using cocaine, and if he had known, he would never have invited me. He had seen firsthand what it had done to my life and was completely against me doing drugs. On my way to the airport, I picked up an eight-ball of cocaine and thought I could use it all weekend without anyone knowing.

I arrived in Vegas on a Friday night and met Ryan and Genie. We all started gambling, then went to dinner and hit some clubs. I managed to control my drinking and cocaine use throughout the night, but when it was time to sleep, I kept snorting cocaine. I would pretend to sleep, then go to the bathroom and do lines. Eventually, I overdid it and got tweaked out, refusing to get off the couch or leave the room for most of the next morning and into the afternoon. Ryan finally confronted me and asked what was wrong, and I told him I was doing cocaine. He got angry and kicked me out of his suite. By that point, I was low on funds because I had gambled most of it away, so I thought I could bet a little more and win enough to get my own room. I sat down at the blackjack table high as hell and drinking heavily, and I had a good run, but by eight o'clock Saturday night, I had lost all my money, with no chance to get more until I returned to Tucson and got paid again. I was in deep trouble because now I had no money, nowhere to stay, and my flight wasn't until Monday afternoon. I had already pawned my watch and lost that money too, and now I had no more cash to gamble or spend on drinks, so I started looking for a solution.

Walking through the parking lot, I looked into cars along the way and noticed a vehicle with a briefcase inside, thinking it might contain something useful. I'm generally not someone who would steal, but at that moment, I was desperate. I grabbed a rock, shattered the window, and took the briefcase. Inside, I found a passport and a checkbook, and I thought I could cash some checks to get some money. By then, feeling desperate and high on alcohol and cocaine, I had no moral compass to guide me and convince me that what I was doing was wrong. I was in survival mode and didn't care who I hurt or the consequences. My pride kept me from calling my best friend, apologizing, and humbling myself to ask for help. Had I done that, he would still have been angry, but he would have helped me. We are brothers.

So instead, I started forging checks, pretending to be the guy on the passport. Every time I got money, I would end up gambling it away. I would cash a check, then go to the casino to gamble and drink until I lost everything, doing this all night until I was broke. I had forged checks at all the places and around the casino. The Rio is not on the main Las Vegas Strip; it's on the other side of the highway from most of the major casinos. I was drunk and looking for a way to cross over to the main strip to write more checks when I found a Rio Casino maintenance golf cart. Aha! Here's my new ride. I jumped inside and started driving away. I went down the street, off the property, crossed the highway, and headed to the famous Las Vegas Strip. Once there, I started racing down the sidewalk recklessly, weaving through pedestrians in front of the hotels and casinos. What a sight that must have been for the spectators! I don't remember which casino I stopped at, but at one point, I parked the golf cart and went inside to cash one of the stolen checks. I still don't know how or why I wasn't arrested along the way. I was reckless, driving a stolen casino golf cart down the Las Vegas Strip, drunk and high, with people jumping out of my way, and everyone looking at me like I was crazy. Bad boys, bad boys, Whatcha gonna do? Whatcha gonna do when they come for you?

Inside the casino, a lady questioned my passport and said I didn't look like the man in the photo. I quickly explained that I had lost a lot of weight because I have leukemia, which threw her off my trail, and I was able to cash a check for about $500, enough to get a room. I left the casino and jumped into a cab, heading for Mandalay Bay. I bought a room, took a shower, and settled in, knowing I was about to go gambling. The thing with me and my addiction is that I can use many different substances to get high. If not alcohol, then cocaine. If not cocaine, then gambling or anything that gives me a rush and changes how I feel. This time, it was all three combined, making a deadly mix. It's Sunday, early afternoon, and I've been awake since Friday morning, drinking alcohol and snorting cocaine, and I'm still going strong. Now, adrenaline from gambling is my focus. I went down to the casino floor, sat at the blackjack table, and started playing — I was on fire! About five hours later, I was up nearly $4,000, and I decided to leave the table, go back to my room, and get ready for a wild night out, Vegas style, with all the money I had just won. I had huge plans to hit the strip club, buy more cocaine, and party like a rock star until my flight leaves.

It's Sunday night, and I've showered and gotten ready for a long night of partying. I was leaving the casino to catch a cab to the strip club when the blackjack table started calling my name. It was urging me to come back and try again, to turn that $4,000 into $10,000, and I believed the voice. I sat down, thinking I was about to hit it big, but I lost all my money—except my last $100. I figured if I walked away from the table with $100, that would be enough to get me to the airport the next day to catch my flight home. Feeling dejected and angry at myself for losing the money, I finally gave up and accepted that my run was over. I went to my room and passed out, only to wake up just in time to catch my flight back to Tucson. My friend was understandably pissed, and my pregnant girlfriend back home had no idea what my weekend had been like because I didn't tell her. They say what happens in Vegas stays in Vegas, and I was sticking to that rule—keeping everything about my crazy weekend secret. That was how I operated during my addiction—doing things completely out of character and then hiding them, hoping no one would find out. Over time, this built up like baggage, and soon everything would come crashing down—much like stacking a deck of cards until the weight was too much and the whole house of cards collapsed. So too would my life. My addiction had eroded my character, leading me to break laws, lie, cheat, steal, and mistreat people—selling them out for my drink and drugs every time.

It's March 2000, and my girlfriend, Kara, who later becomes my wife, is pregnant with our daughter, Brooke. She already has a four-year-old son, Brandon. I am preparing to start a family and become a father. You might think this would be enough to motivate me to finally be honest with myself and take action about my addiction. Surely, this could serve as a catalyst for change. You would think that someone about to become a dad would clean up? Nope, not me! Once again, I refused to admit that I was an alcoholic and a drug addict and thought I could never drink or use drugs again. In my mind, I was afraid I couldn't live without them and their comfort. I truly believed that if I just worked harder and tried something different, I could enjoy both alcohol and crack cocaine recreationally, like I saw others do. The problem is, as my sister Missy once told me, "Michael, there is no such thing as a recreational crack smoker, and you are not going to be the first!" No truer words have ever been spoken than these. LOL!

In Tucson, my addiction got very bad! My disappearing acts became longer, and now I was not just hurting myself and my immediate family members; I was now hurting my children and abandoning the new family that I was supposed to be leading. The shame and guilt were almost unbearable, knowing what I was doing to the people who were counting on me the most, and the fact that my children were missing their daddy and were wondering why I had left them and would not come home. It is an absolute nightmare to be high on crack and the thoughts of your children tugging at your soul. One time in Tucson, I was high in the parking lot of an apartment building, and I began to have delusional hallucinations. When I would look up at the apartments, I could see my children looking out the windows at me, and they were crying and being held against their will, and I couldn't do anything about it but sit there in terror, telling myself that it wasn't real. I had many such occasions like this when my soul nearly cracked, and my mind almost came unraveled entirely, where the shame and guilt were so severe, and it was strangling the life from my being. It was that terrible. Once I opened up my mind to the enemy by smoking drugs, I was easy prey for countless mind games all bent on driving me crazy and trying to get me to act out and destroy myself and others.

Another time in Tucson, I was getting high in an apartment located in a complex overrun by drugs. When I smoke crack, most of the time, I get very paranoid. This time, there was a gangbanger in the apartment, and he was walking around looking out the windows, waving his pistol in the air, saying he was going to shoot someone. His street name was "Regulator," and everyone was scared of him because he often acted erratically, threatening and bullying people. At one point, I left the apartment I was in to get some more crack, and "Regulator" was outside. As I walked across the complex, he approached me and barked loudly in my ear like a dog. The gang he was associated with called themselves 'Dogs or Mad-Dogs'. This made me angry, but I was too high and paranoid to do anything, so I kept walking and returned to the original apartment. I sat down on the couch and waited for the high to wear off so I wouldn't be so paranoid and scared. Once the high faded, I went outside again to find "Regulator," and I saw him in the street, surrounded by his homeboys who watched as I approached. I walked up to him, squared up, and said, "You bark like a puppy, 'ruf-ruf,' but I bark like this, 'WOOF-WOOF.'" I mimicked the ruf-ruf quietly like a squeaky little puppy, then yelled the WOOF-WOOF loudly, like a real dog. I then punched him in the jaw, and the fight was on. I took it to him, and he went down. When he got back up, he started running away. His homeboys watched as "Regulator' ran off. I yelled, "I'm the Big Dog up in here!" and then headed back to the apartment. I kept smoking. That day, I gained some respect around there. Rumors spread quickly about what that "White-Boy" had done to the "Regulator." After that, "Regulator" stayed far away from me. The following week, I was in another apartment, and one of the guys there started freestyling about my fight with the "Regulator." I wish I still had the words to that rap!

There was always something wild and crazy happening with me when I started to drink alcohol, then go and smoke crack. This same old pattern repeated itself over and over again. It is like the tide of an ocean, when the tide goes out—you know, without a doubt, it is going to come flooding back in. Just give it a little time. When I started drinking, you knew without a doubt that the flood of a crack cocaine relapse was just a matter of time, and then I would be gone. You could set your watch to it because it was that predictable. Everyone saw this pattern except me. I was blind back then. It's interesting to me that the house we moved into in Tucson was on a street named Snakeroot. This turned out to be prophetic because it was during this time that the snake rooted itself deep in my soul and injected me with the dark poison of crack cocaine addiction. It got brutal!

It's April 2005, and I have gone missing again. I'm running wild through the streets of Tucson, stealing liquor from grocery stores and selling it on the black market to fund my drug habit. I would push a grocery cart into the store, fill it with gallon bottles of premium liquor, then sneak out with it. Most of the time, I'd get away unnoticed, but sometimes, they would try to stop me. When that happened, I'd either fight them and escape or get caught, with the police called, a ticket issued, or me sent to jail. If I went to jail, I'd stay about six days, get time served, and be right back out on the streets doing the same thing. I had lost my car, so I was walking, riding the bus, or hitching a ride with whoever would give me a lift. That evening, I was riding with another crack user named Slim, and he took me to the grocery store so I could steal some liquor. This time, I didn't go unnoticed. Three large employees grabbed me at the door, body-slammed me, and held me down until the police arrived. When the officer got there, he issued a citation for shoplifting the booze and for the crack pipe in my pocket, then let me go. My ride had taken off when he saw me being dragged to the ground, so I took off on foot down the street when the police said I could go. I was hyped up on adrenaline and ready for some action. As I was walking fast through the streets, leaving the area where I stole the liquor, I started yelling at the top of my lungs, "I'm Money-Mike and I will not be denied, I'm Money-Mike and I will not be denied!" I would say this over and over, screaming through the streets of Tucson. I'm not sure where that came from, but I was rolling with it at the time.

I made a block and turned onto a main road through Tucson called Speedway, then started moving quickly. I was determined not to go home empty-handed and was looking for my next move. I walked into a bar and went into the bathroom, scoping out the bar to see if there was any opportunity that I could steal something. I didn't see anything, so I left the bar through the front door and headed through the parking lot, which was full of cars. At this point, I was in complete crazy mode. I came across a red Roush Mustang convertible with the top down parked outside the bar. Instinctively, as if another force was controlling me, I opened the door that was left unlocked and jumped into the driver's seat. I immediately reached into the middle console and retrieved the car key, as if it were waiting for me to arrive. Vroom! I started this racecar I had found and took off into the night. This was the first car I had ever stolen in my life, and I couldn't believe I was doing it at the time. As you read this book, you will see the significance of the first car I ever stole being a Mustang.

I drove about a mile back to where Slim and I had started our crime spree and pulled into the parking lot, screeching my tires and honking the horn while the music blared at full volume. The look on Slim's face when I pulled up to his apartment was one of astonishment and complete disbelief. He said to me, "I saw you get caught and thought you went to jail, and now you show up 30 minutes later in a race car, I don't believe what I am seeing!" This was an extraordinary series of events, and it only got stranger.

The following week, I stayed in the car and started to believe it was mine. I was completely out of my mind, high on cocaine and adrenaline during a manic episode unlike any before or since. I found a bunch of credit cards in the trunk of the Mustang and spent the week running them up to pay for the steady stream of crack that kept fueling this madness. Sometime after the first week with the car, I was in a neighborhood called "South Park" in South Tucson, looking to score some crack, when an undercover police car pulled me over. I was stopped at a stop sign when he pulled up behind me, activating his dashboard lights. He got out of his car and approached me, telling me to pull over to the side of the road. The top was down, and I had two other people with me in the car. I told them to get out, and they did. Then, I pulled the car over to the side of the road. The unmarked police officer parked his vehicle in front of mine to prevent me from moving forward.

The officer approached my car and asked who it belonged to, and I told him it was mine. The words came out of my mouth so quickly, I think I believe it by now. Then he asked me to hand over my driver's license, and I did, as if there was no problem at all. Then it hit me like a ton of bricks. "Oh crap, I am going to go to jail." I made a split-second decision and said, 'No, I am not,' then put the car in reverse, floored it, skidded the car in the other direction, and took off. This is a Roush Mustang, which is by far the fastest car I have ever driven, equipped with a racing suspension. I was out of there, and there was no way he was going to catch me. I got away and headed to the North side to hide for a bit. I was panicked and full of adrenaline after the high-speed chase, but now I knew I would be wanted for the stolen vehicle, the credit cards, and fleeing and evading. At this point, I told myself I would drive this thing until the wheels fell off, and they could try to catch me if they could. I was on the run!

I lay low for a few days, then one evening I backed into a 7-Eleven while waiting for my dealer to bring me some crack and saw a girl crying on the phone. She was working in Tucson for one of those "door-to-door" sales companies and staying in Phoenix, and her ride left her stranded in Tucson. Phoenix is 115 miles away, or about a two-hour drive, so I decided to take her there. I knew they were looking for me in Tucson, so heading to Phoenix was a smart move.

I dropped her off in Phoenix, and she gave me twenty dollars for gas. Then I headed out to find some crack. I knew I had to get more money, so I went to a liquor store and backed the car into a parking space near the door. It was about eleven at night, and the place was empty except for one guy at the register. I walked in, grabbed two bottles of Patron Tequila, and then headed for the Mustang. I threw the bottles in the back seat and jumped into the car. I turned the key and started the engine when suddenly the clerk appeared out of nowhere, pointing a 45mm pistol at me and shouting, "Get out of the car!" I looked at him and said, "Not for no liquor you're not," then hit the gas and peeled out of the parking lot with my stolen bottles of tequila. I was lucky he didn't shoot me. Thank you, Jesus!

I traded the liquor for crack and kept smoking. Later that morning, I met a crack dealer, and we started riding in the Mustang together. At first, I was driving, but then I let him take over so I could smoke. That evening, after a long day, we ended up at a trap house, which is a place where many people go to smoke crack, sharing their crack with the owner as payment for being there. I had been up for about a week at this point, and my body finally gave out, and I passed out in the house. When I woke up the next day, my watch was gone from my wrist, and my stolen red Roush Mustang had vanished. I was pissed and angry, wanting to fight someone. I yelled at the people inside and then left to try to find the Mustang or steal another car. Keep in mind, I'd never stolen a car before, but since I stole the first one, I had become an auto thief and no longer cared about the consequences.

I hit the streets, and within an hour, I walked up to a Circle K convenience store just as a guy went inside and left his red Mitsubishi 3000GT running, because it was so hot that day. I jumped in and drove off. Then I did what I usually did—boosted more liquor—and once I loaded up, I returned to that crack house where I lost the Mustang to see if by chance the guy who took it was around, and I could punch him in the mouth. He wasn't there, so I grabbed a gallon bottle of Absolute Vodka and threw it through their living room window, yelling that they were all punks. Full-blown anger, mania, and insanity poured from every pore of my body, and euphoria took over me, transforming me into a completely different person. A lunatic out of control. I had entered the realm of madness, losing all touch with reality and who I was. I had become a menace to society, hell-bent on keeping this runaway crazy train rolling strong—with cocaine, booze, adrenaline, and adventure. I didn't want to stop. I think, on some level, I knew I had gone too far, and I was going to pay big time for this one, so I was determined to squeeze every last bit of what I had out of it until there was nothing left.

For about a week, it was business as usual with a steady supply of alcohol and crack to keep me going. I made friends at another trap house and used it as my base of operations. One afternoon, a couple showed up with a big bag of crystal meth. I had tried some before, but I preferred crack. By then, I was willing to try anything, so I started snorting and smoking large amounts, and I got incredibly wired. I stayed in the trap house, using meth all day, late into the night, and through the early morning. I finally decided the apartment was too small and that the world needed to see me; that was a bad idea. I shot out of that apartment like a Roman candle on the Fourth of July, with another guy in tow, and we went looking for more crack. We visited our usual spots, but around four in the morning, everyone was out of drugs. Leaving one dealer's spot, I rolled up to a stop sign, and a Phoenix police officer drove right past me on Van Buren Street, a known area for crime and drugs. The guy in my car told me to turn left and drive the opposite way from the cop, but I refused because I thought that would look suspicious. Instead, I turned to the right and followed him—a huge mistake. I kept going straight when he made a right, and I was home free!

I made a quick turn into the next neighborhood to leave Van Buren Avenue and shake off the cop. I looked in my rearview mirror and told the guy in my car that we had escaped him. Out of nowhere, the cop lit me up, and the chase was on. The guy next to me was yelling at me to stop, and I told him no way—he would have to jump out. I was driving through the streets of Phoenix, trying to lose the cop, and after a few minutes, I saw two more police cars joining the chase. I was running red lights, blowing through intersections, and doing a pretty good job of keeping the cops off my tail. I noticed I was pulling away from them a bit and thought it was because of my driving skills, but what I didn't realize was that they had fallen back because the helicopter had me targeted. I told the guy in the car to get ready to jump out when I made my next left, and he prepared himself. I slowed down and took the turn at about 20 MPH, and he jumped out and rolled a bit, then got up and ran. He managed to escape. I kept driving and decided to do the same. I believed I could jump out of the car while it was moving, and the vehicle would continue forward, letting me escape while they followed the stolen car. The meth mind will believe anything is possible. I picked my spot and jumped out at 20 MPH. As soon as I jumped out, instead of going straight, the vehicle immediately turned right and crashed into a parked van. I knew I had to get out of there quickly, so I hit the ground running and headed into the houses. I jumped a fence, ran through a backyard, jumped another fence, then another, and through the backyard, and now I was on the next street. By then, my legs were exhausted, and I had no idea how I would get over the next fence.

 Running as fast as my legs would go, I crossed the street and approached the next fence, then decided to run and break through the gate. I hit the gate at full speed, knocked it off the hinges, and made my way through the yard. I will never forget what happened next. As I made my turn around a corner in the yard, the spotlight from the helicopter lit up the entire yard, and as I was making the corner, I saw a dog sitting up calmly, like he was expecting me, and the dog just watched me as I ran by. I thought this was very peculiar at the time, as most dogs would be frightened and run away, or they would attack. This dog just sat there, as if he were enjoying the show and had been waiting for me to arrive. I skirted by the dog and made my way to the back fence, jumped it, and as I did, I heard a cop yell, 'Freeze.' I shouted back at him, "F#@%" you, and made a turn down the alley because my legs were too tired to jump another fence. I was running down the alley, which was now lit up like a football stadium by the helicopter's spotlight, and running directly at an oncoming police car moving quickly in my direction. I'm not sure what I was thinking I was going to do once we reached the collision point, but I did not have to worry about it because before I could reach impact with the cop car, two huge and powerful Phoenix police officers tackled me and slammed me to the ground. No touchdown for me on this run! They held me down and roughed me up a bit as I continued to resist. I could not breathe at this point and felt like I was about to die as more officers showed up and piled on. At one point, one of the officers called everyone off, and the area became calm, and I finally gave up the fight. Later, as I sat in the back of the police car, one of the officers told me how lucky I was because of the way I was fighting; they usually use more force. He said the guy who called off the extra force was a Christian, and that I was lucky. Thank you again, Jesus!

After I was taken to the police station, I found myself experiencing a severe methamphetamine and cocaine psychosis. I was in a holding cell and could hear people's thoughts, or at least I thought I could. They took me for evaluation, as they always do when you're booked into jail, especially after arrests like mine. I told the officer that I thought it was cool how the other inmates could all communicate telepathically with their thoughts. I said I could read their minds and hear what they were thinking. He looked at me like I was crazy and then told me I needed some time alone. Then he walked me down the hallway and put me in a separate holding room. My mind was racing, and I could hear voices in my head as I started to panic. I remember feeling very scared, thinking I had driven myself crazy and was now a schizophrenic, and that I was going to end up in a mental institution. That's when I heard a new voice in my head say, "Michael, it's just the drugs…Michael, it's just the drugs." This calmed me down, and I began repeating out loud what I was hearing in my mind, and instantly, the voices disappeared, and my psychosis was gone. I believe Jesus was delivering me from the insanity and bringing peace to my mind and soul. I was utterly insane, then the good Word, which is Truth, came to me: "Michael, it's just the drugs," and in that moment, I came to my senses and was set free. Thank you once again, Jesus!

I was booked and spent the following fourteen months in Maricopa and Pima County jails. I served seven months in Maricopa County for fleeing and evading in a stolen red Mitsubishi 3000GT, and another seven months in Pima County for fleeing and evading in a stolen red Roush Mustang. I'm not sure how I managed to avoid prison on this one. I had been on the run for about a month from the time I stole the Mustang in Tucson until I crashed the Mitsubishi in Phoenix. In the Maricopa County Jail, I spent the first few months in the central detention facility, where I saw a lot of violence. Our housing unit included a day room with two televisions, a recreational area with a basketball hoop, and two tiers of cells that could hold around 100 inmates.

One night, they brought a new inmate into our cell block, and immediately, people started talking about him. He took his things to his cell, and the word went out that he was a Catholic Priest who had been in the news for molesting young boys. In jail and prison, there is a green light for all people who have committed crimes against children as part of the jail and prison culture. A green light means you are to fight that person and do as much damage as you can to them before the guards get in there and break it up. If you end up in a cell with a person who is in there because they have committed a crime against a child, and you do not fight him, then the other prisoners will come and beat you up for not initiating a green light. The beating serves as retribution for the crime committed against the innocent child, where the child was unable to protect themselves from the predator. The idea behind it is that now the person who committed the crime against the child becomes the prey, and the prison inmates are the predators. Street justice, if you will.

I will never forget what happened next. A group of inmates went into the cell and started assaulting this man, and it was bad. You could hear the thumps on his skull throughout the cell block. When I went over to see what was going on, I saw three men jumping up and down on the guy's head and blood all over the floor. They were stomping him to death. After a little while, the three men exited the cell, leaving the injured man in there, bleeding and dying. About 5 minutes later, the jail guards rushed in to secure the area, and then the medical personnel came in and wheeled the bloodied man out on a hospital gurney. I thought the guy was dead. The medical team put up caution tape around the cell to protect the crime scene. Then the guards lined up all the inmates along the wall for a knuckle-check. If you had red on your knuckles, they would put you in cuffs and carry you to Ad Seg, which is Administration Segregation, for prisoners with behavioral problems who cannot follow the rules or commit crimes while incarcerated. If you go to Ad Seg, it is a terrible place to be, and you will likely be there for a very long time. I know this first-hand because I got caught making "Hooch", prison alcohol made from fruit, bread, and sugar, and ended up in Ad Seg myself. The time I went to Ad Seg, I had my hair cut into a mohawk as an act of rebellion. I was a wild man back then. This time in jail, I was not seeking God, but just becoming a worse drug addict and criminal.

After spending two months in the central detention facility, they transferred me to Sheriff Joe Arpaio's Tent City, an outdoor area in the desert where inmates lived in old army tents. Man, was it hot. Temperatures sometimes soared above 110 degrees during the day. We received pink underwear, pink socks, and pink sheets as part of the punishment. I guess the Maricopa County Sheriff thought it would be humiliating for us inmates. The pink clothes and bedding didn't bother us much, but the heat was nearly unbearable. People often fainted from heat exhaustion, especially the older inmates and those with other medical issues. The facility was eventually closed in 2017 due to high costs and concerns about inhumane conditions. Luckily, I was able to leave after five months and finish my time in Pima County in a facility with air conditioning.

After being released from jail, I was placed on Intensive Probation, which is similar to house arrest for another year, followed by three more years of regular probation. I entered a halfway house and eventually moved into an apartment. I was doing the weekend dad thing and feeling like a failure in my life.

I wanted my family back, but I didn't stay clean and sober long enough to make that happen.

Completing intensive probation was very challenging, but I successfully finished my year and was then placed on regular probation. I didn't last long and soon went back to smoking crack. The apartments I lived in at the time had drug activity, and as soon as I had some freedom, I sought it out. I relapsed, absconded from probation, and went on the run again. I am using crack cocaine daily with little or no sleep or food, and I meet up with a woman who claims to be a witch and practices Wicca, a modern pagan witchcraft religion. She tells me she is part of a coven of witches, and they are all going to meet, and she wants me to come along. We go to this house, owned by a man who is a warlock, and we start using drugs. In the main room, a large fireplace burns with a fire, and a big, round coffee table is surrounded by couches. In the room, there is a statue of a witch crouched in a sitting position, her face down toward the ground, with only her pointed hat and the outline of her body visible. On the other side of the room, there is a statue of an Indian head, painted with incredible detail. We are getting high, and at one point, the warlock looks at me and says, "It is better to reign in hell than it is to serve in Heaven." This was very unsettling, but I was extremely high, so I shrugged it off and kept getting high. Some time passed, and more people arrived, whom I believe were the coven she mentioned. Everyone gathered around the big, round table, and I joined them.

Each took a turn smoking crack, and the pipe was passed around, with me being the last to take a hit. Once I did, I immediately entered a terror-stricken panic mode, ran to the back door of the house, opened it, and placed one foot outside and one inside the house, pressing my back against the door frame. I stood at the door with my head moving back and forth from left to right, looking outside the house, then inside, then outside again, as the spiritual realm of wickedness began its attack. I couldn't see them with my physical eyes, but I perceived some spiritual beings flying in and out of the house through the door I had just opened. They would fly past me quickly, entering and exiting through the door, and I would try to follow them with my head. I was absolutely terrified and panic-stricken, feeling that I was engaging with something profoundly wicked. It was strange to me that I knew I was acting very weird at the door, but nobody in the room was even looking at me. That did not make sense. I know that if I saw someone acting the way I was acting then, I would definitely be staring at them, wondering what their problem was. But they did not even take a peek. At one point, the woman who had brought me there said to the others, and I will never forget this, "He is just not used to these kinds yet." That has always stayed with me, as I believe I was experiencing, for the first time, the evil spirit of a witch. It's a common myth that witches leave their bodies at night to fly away, either to meet with other witches or to steal the lives of their victims. I can't confirm for sure that this was what I experienced, but I can share the facts and describe what happened, and let you decide the truth for yourself.

Later that evening, after everyone had left or fallen asleep, I was alone in the main room with the fireplace and round table. I wandered around in a drug-induced daze, staring intently at the Indian head statue and noticing its mesmerizing details. I looked very hard and became lost in the moment when I saw a tear fall from one of the statue's eyes, streaming down its cheek. In that instant, I took a couple of quick, shallow breaths and then felt something enter me. Then I started dancing around the room barefoot, like an Indian war dance, singing Indian chants and moving to the beat of an internal drum. I was lost in the moment, and this continued for a few minutes until I dropped my glass crack pipe; it shattered on the floor. I stepped on it and cut my foot. I immediately snapped back to myself and the reality of my surroundings, ran to the laundry room, and grabbed a white towel because my foot was bleeding badly. I wiped away the blood, which covered the towel, and I began to panic, now believing that the witches would take my blood and use it against me in some spell to do harm. I was what they call in the drug world, "On-One!"

Time passed, and I eventually settled down, falling asleep after about six or seven days of being awake with no food, little water, and lots of crack smoking.

I bear witness to this encounter with the spiritual realm, and I know many readers of this book have experienced similar situations where using certain substances under the right conditions opened them up to a strange and startling spiritual realm, leaving them unprotected and unprepared for what would follow. The alcohol and drugs we consume serve as seeds of spiritual wickedness, making us vulnerable to evil and unclean spirits from the demonic kingdom of darkness. Over time, if these seeds are not rooted out and destroyed, they will grow and choke out any good seed of God, filling our souls with darkness instead of light and bringing us under the control of the devil, turning us into slaves to his weapon of addiction. When this happens, we become easily manipulated by evil forces and unclean spirits that now move freely through our souls because of the portal we've opened with drugs. Our souls are under attack, and our bodies—designed to be temples of God—are being prostituted and playing the harlot. Demons and unclean spirits (strangers) pass through, defiling our bodies and using them for wickedness.

JOEL 3:17 (KJV)

So shall ye know that I am the LORD your god dwelling in Zion, my holy mountain: then shall Jerusalem be holy, and there shall no stranger's pass through her any more.

This is as serious as it gets, folks! Messing with drugs is like a toddler playing with a hand grenade. He throws it around the room, thinking it's harmless fun because of its cool, funny-looking shape, and he mistakes it for a toy. That's what we do when we experiment with drugs—we think they're fun and exciting. The same thing applies to us as it does to that toddler. One wrong pull of the pin, and boom—lights out! The harsh truth is that both are made to kill and destroy. If you keep using drugs, you will become addicted and ultimately be destroyed. The drugs will corrupt your mind, soul, and body, turning you into a servant of sin and the devil. You will be chained to drugs like a slave. If you sell drugs, you are an instrument of evil, working with the devil and helping the enemy destroy lives. God issues a strong warning in His Word to those who lead others into sin. When we sell drugs to people, we are encouraging them to sin. In my addiction, I both used and sold drugs. I was hopelessly addicted and found myself turning into someone I never thought I would be. I hated the person I had become.

MATTHEW 18:6 (NKJV)
"Whoever causes one of these little ones who believe in me to sin, it would be better for him if a millstone were hung around his neck, and he were drowned in the depth of the sea.

Soon after my experience of smoking drugs with witches, I was caught by the Tucson police for selling a twenty-dollar crack rock to an undercover officer. They eventually grew tired of my antics and sentenced me to two and a half years in the Arizona Department of Corrections. I spent the first year at the Florence Unit before being transferred to the Marana Facility near Tucson. This was a relief because it was close to my children, and they could visit me. It's a sad day when you haven't seen your kids in over a year, and the first time you see them is in a prison visitation room. Oh, Michael Bowen, look how far you've fallen. Oh, Michael Bowen, look at what your life has become. You had the world in your hands with endless opportunities, and you threw them all away, becoming a complete failure. This message haunted me in the back of my mind, like a broken record repeating itself over and over. I kept hearing it, and I couldn't stop it. Look at what you wasted and threw away for crack. You are a stupid man. You're weak and selfish, and everyone sees you as a loser. It's hard when you have to agree with that voice and realize how selfish and destructive you've been, hurting everyone you love, including those who love you the most. The hardest part is holding on to the tiny shred of belief that you're still a good person when everything screams otherwise. I always clung to that small piece of truth. Michael, it's just the drugs; you are a good person.

Throughout my addiction in Tucson from 1999 to 2009, I experienced periods of sobriety. Although they were brief, I had good stretches with positive results. I completed several successful sales jobs in telecommunications, took my children on memorable vacations, attended church regularly for a time, coached my oldest son's flag football team, and experienced moments of clarity and closeness to God. However, these victories were always temporary. They were quickly overshadowed by another descent into the dark and dangerous world of crack cocaine, filled with dark magic, wickedness, and insanity. It was hard for me to keep going after falling so many times, only to get back up and fall again. A normal person might have given up, but I kept fighting because that's just who I am. I don't have any quit in me—sometimes to my detriment, but in this case, I believe it helped me. "I fight because I am strong, and I am strong because I fight." That is a motto I live by. I credit my perseverance in this journey through addiction to my football training and the lessons it taught me about toughness and never quitting—always getting back up when knocked down. These lessons were essential in surviving this deadly game I was playing with crack cocaine, where there are no cheering crowds, no awards, and no accolades—only captivity, darkness, and hell of addiction.

SEEDS

Seeds of wickedness
Sown in the drugs you use
Evil spirits hidden
In the substances you abuse
Deception from the enemy
Hidden right under your nose
As you partake in pleasure
The angry demons grow
The devil uses a lie
Recreation as a scheme
Get you hooked on fun and excitement
Get you carried away in a dream
Then one day
Once the evil has comfortably settled in
You are caught in a trap
Addiction is now your friend
A love hate relationship
Always destruction in the end
A broken heart and beaten body
Wounded spirit taken by the wind
Witches spell dark magic potion
Iron feet caught in shameful mire
Now your whole pitiful life
Whittled down to one selfish desire
Where can I get more
How can I get higher
Gone all the fun and excitement
Out of the frying pan into the fire
The angry demons are never satisfied
Without any legs trying to run
Painfully you search for an answer

To a question that will never yield one
The enemy now has you guarded
Protected in his garden of sin
Only you in full bloom and wickedness
Your drug and desire your only friends
The loneliness of addiction
The devil having his destroying way
Stealing from you your loved ones
Caught in this wicked game you must play
Now you must make a decision
Today it takes a certain choice
Cry out now for your savior
Be quick to listen to His saving voice
Faithfully He will answer
Jesus always delivers from sin
Reach for the hand he gives you
The loving hand of a trusted friend
Say goodbye forever to your addiction
Now you are hand in hand with the son
Cast out those angry demons
In the name of Jesus this is done
Rest now in the arms of your savior
There He will heal your soul
In Him you are victorious
Through Him you will shine as gold
Become His precious vessel
In you now new seeds are sown
Seeds of good and righteousness
Bearing sweet fruit when they are grown
No longer will you ponder
The answers to questions unknown
Now your eyes have opened
The garden of wisdom is your home
Now you are that good soil

You are that seed that Jesus has sown
Life giving water nourishes
Mighty tree standing tall never alone
For God is always with you
Walking by your side in His garden each day
Now when the seeds of wickedness come
Let Jesus take them away
He will conquer all of your enemies
In Him they will be placed under your feet
Arise, stand firm in victory
Remembering, the fruit is always in the seed!

CRACK IS WACK

Crack is whack
There is no way back
A certain heart attack
Fall for a dummy sack
Once you let the beast in
Crack will lead you into sin
Always a loser never a win
The rock is now your only friend
No time to scream and shout
The monster has found its way out
The pipe a never-ending drought
Now your name carries no clout
If you don't want to lose
And stop selling your last pair of shoes
No more singing the cocaine blues
You better move to choose
Say no to the rock
Stop walking the streets in your socks
Put an end to making the block
Get your head and hands out of iron stocks
Just say no to the wind
When crack calls to her lonely friend
Turn on your heels and spin
Get ghost and flee from sin
Crack is whack

VALLEY OF DECISION

Wings of flowing cherubim
Standing tall layered feather gold
Spirit fire-breathing heart
Usher in the ancient of old
Mighty talon fighter
Iron eagle claw
Bronze bow at full bend
River of angels, my spirit eyes opened saw
Room on fire is now breathing
Teaming with life the wicked soon to be found out
Angel battalions marching
Pouring into the room like water from a spout
Valley of Decision is forming
Purple robe looks on from afar
His shine has been compromised
Evil has crept into one of His jars
A vessel made for righteousness
Made to overflow with glorious joy
Demons through smoke have invaded
Giant sword strikes consecrated soil
Seeds of loathsome wickedness
Unable to take their root
Oh, Mighty Army of God
Cherubim fight eye for eye tooth for tooth
Oh, Heavenly Battalion
Full battle armor reflecting His shine
King of Kings looks forward
Defeated enemy eyes rewind
Running back to division
Nowhere here left to reside
Demon retreats through a failing wall

The ceiling no place to hide
Gone all the cowardly wickedness
Spit out demon in front of the fiery host
Angels in aqueducts unrelenting
Cherubim legions come by way of the Holy Ghost
Great Army of God defended
Valley of Decision handled with light
Michael Bowen our fellow soldier
We brought you here to help you in your fight
Now you know we are with the Spirit that is within you
Wherever in the physical the Lord has you to go
We are His strength when you need us
We are always ready to show
Now as you march onward
Wherever you are sent to faithfully serve our King
Now you know the Power
The Power behind the mighty Sword you swing!

PEANUTS FOR SALE

Peanuts for sale
The clowns come dancing in
Circus of the Absurd
Trapeze artists flying through smoked, filled winds
Life under the big top
Quite a spectacle for all
Another fall into addiction
An elephant walking on a bright red ball
Tigers fiercely acting
Fooled by the lion tamer's whip
Deeper into the illusion
Another head first dive into addiction after a slip
Baby pool of cement
No water to break the high dive fall
The crowd locked in astonishment
Man on stilts standing tall
Alone at the bottom of the ladder
The crowd's cheers lifting your climb back to the top
Another fall to the hardness
One more tormenting belly flop
Addiction again makes a mockery
The fat lady never sings
Monkeys playing baseball
Only more laughter your continued failures bring
All has gone to darkness
The fire blows on the performer's mighty breath
Addiction has you captivated
Leading you boldly into sure death
Horses prancing in a circle
Woman with a long flowing beard
The lions have forgotten their power

The days gone by when they were once feared
So too are you in your addiction
All have fallen for the ringmaster's lie
Animals do it for the food
The addict does it for the high
Circle full of confusion
Trained eyes unable to see through the smoke
Addiction is a distorted mirror
A fun house full of laugh in your face jokes
The devil has you captured
Like the ringmaster pride-fully on his stand
Serving him for his pleasure
Lost in the chaos of the big top marching band
Drums beating in lopsided rhythm
Big horn tuba blaring just off the note
Pretty girls dancing forward
Spinning batons high in the air as they float
Caught in the performing moment
Addiction has you playing the leading part
Man riding a unicycle on a tight rope
Dog on two legs in a dress pushing a funny cart
This is the deception
You under a bright light in the middle of the main ring
Sitting alone in a red chair
Your addicted life becoming a scene
Unable to notice around you
The crowd has vanished and the cheering has stopped
All the laughter has gone quiet
The floor from under you has just dropped
Captured again in the silence of darkness
Sitting alone with your drug and no friends
The only smoke now is in your lungs
Into the thin air you now send
Now you are your own spectacle

Addicted life overflowing with sin
The ringmaster has departed
You captured once again by his promising plan
This time he told you it would be different
For you the eye is still not quicker than the hand
Somehow you lost focus
The price for peanuts has just gone up
Broken stilts lay beside you
The tiger's mouth has been wired shut
The big top has come down
All the performers together have left
The circus train has departed
Headed for someplace out west
Now you must take notice
The only circus left in town has tragically become you
How will you stop your addiction
How will you keep the next circus train from coming through
Peanuts for sale
Next time you better not buy
Peanuts in this circus are for the elephants
Addiction is just a big fat lie!

III. MUSTANG PRIDE

JOB 39:19
Have you given the horse strength? Have you clothed his neck with thunder?

PSALM 33:17 (NIV)
A horse is a vain hope for deliverance; despite all its great strength it cannot save

OBADIAH 1:3-4 (NIV)
The pride of your heart has deceived you, you who live in the clefts of the rocks and make your home on the heights, you who say to yourself, 'who can bring me down to the ground?' though you soar like the eagle and make your nest among the stars, from there I will bring you down," declares the LORD.

I JOHN 5:21 (KJV)
Little children, keep yourselves from idols. Amen.

God blesses each of us with gifts to use in advancing His Kingdom and to shine as His beloved children. We are created to become His children of the light, the children of the day, as the scripture says. These God-given gifts are placed within us when God forms us in our mother's womb, meant to be used at an appointed time when God calls us and we discover our purpose in Him. The devil knows this and strives to blind us to our purpose in God and the truth of who we are in Jesus Christ. He uses manipulation, deception, and lies to redirect our God-given gifts toward himself, derailing their purpose and attempting to destroy God's works. The pride of life refers to anything originating from the world that fosters arrogance, self-pride, or boasting. Pride of life arises when we begin to love the world and ourselves within it, building on that love rather than on the love of Jesus Christ from God.

2 TIMOTHY 3:1-5 (NKJV)

But know this, that in the last days perilous times will come: for men will be lovers of themselves, lovers of money, boasters, proud, blasphemers, disobedient to parents, unthankful, unholy, unloving, unforgiving, slanderers, without self-control, brutal, despisers of good, traitors, headstrong, haughty, lovers of pleasure rather than lovers of God, having a form of godliness but denying its power. And from such people turn away!

The devil will try to take our gifts, blessings, and love, deceiving us into using them for evil—serving him, worshipping him, and pursuing the lusts of this world, since he is the ruler of it. He entices us to sin against God. In this tactic, Satan works to convince us that the good from our God-given gifts and blessings should be celebrated as something we've done ourselves, and that we should be proud of our accomplishments. He wants us to puff ourselves up with pride following his example. The first sin ever committed happened in Heaven. God created a host of angelic beings, and the highest-ranking angels were called Archangels, holding positions of great power and authority. There are three Archangels: Michael, responsible for warfare; Gabriel, responsible for delivering messages; and Lucifer, who was responsible for worship. The scripture says Lucifer was perfect and beautiful. At some point, Lucifer saw his beauty, and that's when the first sin entered—pride! In his pride, Lucifer rebelled against God, leading to war in Heaven. He was expelled and fell to the earth like lightning. Now, Lucifer or Satan wants us to sin against God through pride, because he is the father of it.

He tries to deceive us into believing that pleasing men is more important than pleasing a God we cannot see. He whispers that to be relevant in the world; we must perform for it and serve it faithfully to get our reward. The only reward the world offers is empty, self-gratifying words, superficial attention, money for your love and affection, flatteries, or this world's currency of "Atta-boys"! The world cannot give to the spirit and can only satisfy desire in the flesh because the flesh lusts after worldly things. The spirit, on the other hand, longs for the deep things of God. Moreover, as long as you give to the world, it will never be satisfied with what you offer. You always reap what you sow, and if you sow to the world, you will reap its fruitless harvest.

HOSEA 8:7 (NKJV)

They sow the wind, and reap the whirlwind. The stalk has no bud; it shall never produce meal. If it should produce, aliens would swallow it up.

The world always wants more of you. It wants your time, your money, and your talents. The world always screams for more! People who are in love with the world will follow this same pattern and will only love and accept you as long as you continue to give yourself, your service, and the things you possess to them. Stop giving, and you will stop being loved and accepted. They will simply move on to someone else. This may sound harsh to some, but it is the harsh reality of how the world works. Just ask the rich man who has lost all his money or the star high school running back who has blown out his knee, where all their friends have gone. Both our flesh and the world always scream, "Give me more!"

PROVERBS 30:15-16 (NKJV)

The leech has two daughters - give and give! There are three things that are never satisfied, four never say, "enough!": the grave, the barren womb, the earth that is not satisfied with water - and the fire never says, "enough!"

The world, like the flesh, has an unending hunger. As we give the world what it desires, it, in turn, feeds our flesh with what it craves. The world seeks our full attention, productivity, gifts, and blessings directed at it, offering it glory, and it rewards us with things that inflate our pride, as the flesh exalts itself and says, "Hey, would you look at me!" The devil enjoys attacking us through this method of building pride within us. He longs to see us fall, so he encourages us and tempts us to follow him in pride. Satan's fall was caused by pride; in his arrogance, he tried to elevate himself above the stars of God and to become like the Most High. In this rebellion, he was cast out of heaven and sent to the earth, where he now wages war against us. Pride always precedes a fall into destruction, and it was my "Mustang Pride" that went before my fall into my addiction.

PROVERBS 16:18 (NKJV)
Pride goes before destruction and a haughty spirit before a fall.

The wild mustang is an animal I have always identified with due to its nature and symbolism. I admire its strength, speed, emotionality, freedom, and the limitless possibilities of a life spent roaming freely on the open plains. Mustangs are known for their fight-or-flight responses, which are perfect for survival in the wild. They can run like the wind when threatened by predators or stand firm and fiercely fight their enemies. They will run fast and hard when scared or stand up and fight when challenged for dominance within the band, which is a group of horses moving together as a united team. The mustang, to me, is a strong and powerful animal that is sensitive to its environment. It is an animal that has a sense of pride, which helps lead its band to safety and protect its members. For me, Mustang pride was instilled through years of playing football, running up and down the field in pursuit of dominance, and leading my teams to success. I always strived in football to be the best player on my team and to lead us to victory. The Lord blessed me with great athletic ability and gifts suited for football. I was strong, sturdy, agile, fast, tenacious, and I had toughness and fight in me that was unmatched. I did everything to the extreme. It is no coincidence that the mascots of my elementary, high school, and college teams were Mustangs. Coincidence? I think not! The other team mascot was a Warrior when

I was in middle school. Mustang-Warrior, I like the sound of that! It fits my personality well.

I was born to play football. The world has always puzzled and greatly troubled me with its cruelty and confusing ways. From as early as I can remember, I sensed that something was wrong, but I could never quite put my finger on it. Nothing in the world ever made sense, and things always seemed to fall short. To me, the world was not just one plus one equals two. Whenever I added up the numbers, I always got a different answer. I was a very sensitive child with strong emotions and a lot of compassion for others. As I found myself in a world I couldn't understand, I started acting out against it.

At six years old, I broke into the local high school and went on a rage-filled rampage, destroying all the students' art projects. I ransacked the entire room and then stole all the art tools, burying them under one of the portable buildings behind the school. This was very unusual for a child, and I never told anyone about it; it was an action that went unnoticed.

My early childhood was filled with destructive events, and now, as I look back, I see it as an early attempt to lash out at a world that confused, terrified, and infuriated me all at once. On another occasion, I went to a neighbor's house and pulled out all their newly planted bushes because they blocked my path, which I loved to run downhill through across the front yards of my block. Using the downhill slope to increase my speed, I would run like the wind. I loved to run, and I was very fast! My parents spanked my backside for that, as well as for all the other mischievous acts of vandalism and destruction I would commit.

Throughout my childhood, I threw rocks through windows, kicked dents into car doors, broke things, and vandalized the neighborhoods where I lived. I was an enigma; on one hand, I was sweet and compassionate, but on the other, I was angry, pissed off, and ready to fight everything. This inner rage followed me throughout my life. I started repressing my feelings and emotions early on, which is an unconscious denial of overwhelming feelings. I believe I have continued this pattern and still tend to do so today, mainly because of my sensitive nature and the intensity with which I experience my feelings and emotions, both positive and negative. I feel deep empathy and care for the people I meet, and hate trying to navigate all my intense feelings and emotions in the chaotic world raging all around me. It can be a challenging task at times.

I believe I began to stuff my anger early in life as I processed all the injustices, cruelty, and unfairness I saw in the world. The world upset me, confused me, and caused me grief. I couldn't effectively process the overwhelming emotional information flooding into my soul each day. I would suppress my feelings to avoid dealing with their intensity and hide emotions that were too strong for me to express. I was just a young kid with adult-sized feelings, and as a result, I began having behavioral issues at school.

My mother received a call from the school counselor and principal, and we had a meeting where they suggested I see a child psychologist. When I was a child, they didn't have all the medications or detailed diagnoses of childhood development disorders that they have today. The psychologist recommended that my mother keep me busy with as many sports as possible to tire me out. In the 1970s, they didn't instantly label you as hyperactive or attention-deficient and prescribe psych drugs or stimulants. My mother followed the doctor's advice and enrolled me in every sport she could find. I participated in all of them: soccer, baseball, basketball, track, swimming, diving, tennis, and my favorite, football!

As a passionate football lover and dedicated Dallas Cowboys fan from an early age, football was a natural fit for me, and I embraced it eagerly. Before playing organized football, I spent countless hours in our neighborhood, wearing a Cowboys jersey and carrying a football everywhere I went, and playing pickup games with all the other neighborhood kids. I dreamed of becoming the next Roger Staubach, Drew Pearson, or Tony Dorsett. For the first time in my childhood, I was able to channel my bottled-up rage and aggression into the game, using it as an outlet within the rules of play. I fell in love with the physicality of football, the emotional intensity it stirred, and the safe space it provided for expressing those feelings. Hallelujah! I finally found something that made sense to me, and I was in love. I still get butterflies when I recall the early days in elementary school, tearing up and down the field with fiery passion and quickly becoming a star. I was lightning-fast, fearless, full of energy, passionate, and a keen student of the game. I loved the contact and hard hits. I had an inner rage fueling my play that any youth football coach would admire. Naturally, I excelled as an athlete and quickly gained fame as Michael Bowen, the football player.

Football became my sanctuary, my identity, as my whole life revolved around it. Football was the one place in the world where I could escape and be free, where I felt I belonged, and where I could, for a moment, shed the feelings of being different and the hypersensitivity I always carried with me. I fell in love with the game because it became a place where I could experience and react to my inner rage and intense emotions, all at once. I knew only one speed and that was full throttle, baby!

In elementary school, I became the best running back in our youth league, and in sixth grade, I helped lead my team to an undefeated season. It was 1979, and there were 45 seconds left on the clock, and we were playing for the city championship, and we were behind by a few points and on our 28-yard line. I took a direct snap from center, went around the left end, and took it 72 yards for a touchdown to win the game. Throughout middle school and high school, I experienced much of the same success, along with the popularity and accolades that come with being a football star in the state of Texas, where football is King!

In 1985, as a senior at J.J. Pearce High School in Richardson, Texas, a suburb of Dallas, I was one of the top running backs in the state and finished as the second-leading rusher in the Dallas/Fort Worth Metroplex. That year, I earned unanimous All-District 12-5A honors as a running back. I come from a football family. My dad played for Rice University in the late 1950s, and my cousin

Scott Hukabay played for Baylor University. Coincidentally, in 1983, Scott was also a unanimous All-District 12-5A running back for the Plano Wildcats. My older "cuz" was always leading the charge, and I watched him go on to a Division I football school after excelling at the high school level. I was disappointed when no one offered me a scholarship, despite my impressive senior season. I saw guys getting full rides to Division I schools that I faced and had more yards than, and I knew I was better than them. It made me mad! Sure, I was a bit undersized for a running back at 5'8" and 165 pounds, but I was lightning fast, tough as nails, and had proven I could play with the best in high school and shine.

I was being recruited by the University of Tulsa and believed they would offer me a scholarship. I was anxiously awaiting their call as the official college signing day approached, and finally, it arrived. Instead of offering me a scholarship, the coach on the other end of the line told me they had decided to go with a running back who was bigger than I was. That infuriated me, but instead of getting angry and saying something harsh, I calmly told him it was okay because I had decided to join a bigger and better football program than theirs at Southern Methodist University. That shut him up quickly, and it was in that moment that I decided I would be playing my college football in my hometown of Dallas for the SMU Mustangs. Pony-Up Bowen!

After the disappointing recruiting process, during which I was convinced someone would offer me a scholarship, but when they didn't, I felt rejected and unappreciated as a football player. I walked on at SMU in 1986. SMU had always been one of my favorite colleges growing up, and a few years earlier, it had been a national powerhouse with the Pony Express and football stars Eric Dickerson and Craig James. SMU had been put on probation for breaking NCAA rules, so they had no scholarships to offer and relied on walk-on players, which made it a perfect fit for me. When they announced it in the newspaper the following week, they listed me at 6'2" tall, weighing 215 pounds, and I just had to laugh. Oh, my, how many nights I lay in bed wishing I was that size. The irony of it all is quite hilarious. In a way, SMU was telling me the same thing everyone else always told me—you are too small. Oh, man, I was determined to prove them all wrong!

The lack of interest I received from colleges and comments that I was too small to play Division 1 football fueled my inner rage. I showed up on the first day of practice at SMU with a massive chip on my shoulder and something to prove. When I arrived, the guys were huge, but through hard work, complete fearlessness, and a knack for throwing my body into the mix, I worked my way into the starting lineup on special teams. I remember the moment I made the football team. We were sitting in film one morning after a preseason intersquad scrimmage, where I had to play defensive cornerback against the first-team offense, and I had a pretty good scrimmage. At one point, our big fullback took a handoff up the middle, and I sliced through the offensive blockers and hit that dude very hard. I weighed 165 pounds, and he was 245, and I knocked the crap out of him so hard that he went down and had to be taken off the field. Our defensive backs coach, Bill Clay, yelled in the film, "Who was that?" I responded: "Coach, that was me!" Coach Clay yelled back excitedly, "Now that's what I'm talking about, you just made our football team, Bowen!" That was a great moment in my life because it is rare for someone my size and a true freshman to make the travel team. The very first game, on the very first kickoff coverage, I ran down the field and tackled the return man at the 8-yard line. As I came off the field, my coach grabbed me by the facemask and said, "Welcome to the Southwest Conference, Bowen!" It was a great moment because we were playing Rice University in their stadium in Houston, where my dad played on the same field 30 years prior. After this first game, I sat back and said to myself, "You have arrived!"

In 1986, playing college football was a dream come true. All our home games were at Texas Stadium, where I grew up watching my beloved Cowboys on Sundays, and now I was playing on that sacred field myself. We also had away games against Arizona State, Texas,

Baylor, Texas Tech, and Notre Dame, which were life-changing as my world expanded to include the new reality of being a college football player, performing in front of thousands of fans each week, and hearing cheers and admiration for something I excelled at. I had arrived! I performed so well on special teams that season that, when we played the University of Texas, I was named the special teams captain for that game. I still remember walking out for the coin toss, dwarfed between two massive offensive and defensive linemen who were the other two captains. The Texas game happened to be on my birthday, making it a very special day for this kid, who everyone thought was too small to play Division I football. I was playing big-time football and having the time of my life. I was in football heaven!

Later that season, we traveled to Baylor, and I faced my cousin Scott for our only face-to-face meeting, as we were on opposite teams. We were complete opposites. He was over 6 feet tall, weighed more than 240 pounds, and was as strong as an ox. This guy was one of the top shot putters in Texas in high school and could bench press over 400 pounds. It was a matchup of size and brute strength versus speed and quickness, and interestingly enough, when we stepped onto the field for the opening kickoff, we were kicking to them, and he was on kickoff return. As he counted down the line to find out who he was supposed to block, his count stopped on me. It was on, like Donkey Kong! This is lady football at her best, putting cousin against cousin in a monumental collision.

The first time I went down the field, I shook him so hard he fell, and I ran past him to make the tackle. That made the big bear very angry, and it didn't help that I taunted him a bit on the way back to the sideline. The next time down the field, I did the same thing, ran right by him with a smile on my face, but this time the return man broke down the sideline, so I had to adjust and take a cut-off angle in hot pursuit. I had lost sight of Scott until my earhole exploded and the lights went out in Waco! Woo-Hoo! That was the most brutal hit I ever took in my football career, and through poetic justice, it came from my blood and kin, my big "Cuz" Scott Huckabay. Unbeknownst to me, he circled around and, with a big smile of his own, clobbered me with one of the prettiest knockout blows you will ever see in football. It was a "De-Cleater," and once I was hit, all I heard was ringing in my ears, then everything went black. Ouch! When I came to, one of my teammates was helping me off the turf and escorting me back to the sideline. I had no idea where I was or what had happened to me. I had a concussion, but back then, they never used that word. If you took a big hit, you were expected to shake it off and get back in the game, which I did. Back then, football was all about toughness, hard hits, and a never-say-die attitude. After the game, we joked about how great a hit it was and how everyone laughed at me flying through the air. Except my mom; she'd never do such a thing. LOL! My cousin never seemed to get that crooked, cat-ate-the-canary-smile off his face. That night in Waco, the old bull taught the young bull a thing or two as he welcomed me "His Way" to the Southwest Conference.

    The second-to-last game of my freshman year was at Texas Tech, and I had a monster game, earning Special Teams Player of the Game honors. We knew going into that game that our program was in trouble as allegations had begun to surface over potential recruiting violations and rumored player "slush-funds." The game was played on Saturday, November 15, 1986, just three days after Dallas-area sports anchor Dale Hansen's report, called "Pony-Gate," was aired live. Hansen confronted SMU's Athletic Director, Head Football Coach, and the Athletic Director's Administrative Assistant with damning evidence of rules violations and serious program infractions, revealing that an NCAA full investigation was already underway. Our goose was cooked, so to speak, as Hansen provided documentation to prove that the improprieties of the most severe and egregious kind had taken place. We won that game 13-7, but then the following week, we got blown out by Arkansas 41-0, ending the season and what turned out to be the last football game played by SMU until the 1989 season. A few months later, in February 1987, the NCAA gave the SMU football program the so-called "Death Penalty," which shut down the program for what turned out to be two years without games and scholarships, allowing all current football players to be immediately eligible to transfer to other programs. To say I was devastated was an understatement. I had worked so hard to prove the critics wrong who said I was too small to play college football by making the team as a true freshman, and now it was gone!

After the "Death Penalty" was imposed, our team was decimated as top football programs from across the country flooded our campus to recruit the best talent. Once again, I was mostly overlooked. I did receive two scholarship offers, one from Iowa State and the other from Wake Forest. These offers made me feel accomplished and somewhat redeemed after receiving no offers the year before I graduated high school, but my competitive side wanted to play for a national powerhouse. Instead of accepting either offer, I decided to walk on at the University of Georgia. Georgia, at the time, had won a total of five national championships, the latest in 1980. In the fall of 1987, I arrived in Athens, Georgia, with something to prove once again. I joined a talented team in one of the best conferences in the country, the Southeastern Conference. I showed up in great shape and with a significant chip on my shoulder, catching the coaches' attention early and earning a spot in the starting lineup. I learned early in football that with toughness and hard work, you could become a better and more productive player than someone with more raw talent who didn't work as hard. I had a knack for being in the right place at the right time and bringing a hammer on contact. I played fearlessly, flying to the ball as if it were the only thing that could save me. I had no regard for my own body, but my coaches loved my style, intensity, and big heart. That year, I was named the starting punt and kick returner, in addition to my consistent kick-off coverage. We had a great season, finishing 9-3 and winning the Liberty Bowl. I received the Olin Huff Award for the most outstanding walk-on athlete of the year at the University of Georgia, and once again, I made it big on one of college football's biggest stages. Some of my teammates that year included future NFL players: Lars Tate, Keith Henderson, David McCluskey, Rodney Hampton, Mo Lewis, Ben Smith, Tim Worley,

Troy Sadowski, Gary Moss, and the famous professional wrestler "The Monster" Bill Goldberg. All of these players went on to play in the NFL, a league I had also dreamed of joining one day.

As spring football that year started, I began feeling homesick and longed to be back in Dallas with my friends and family. I had a successful spring football camp and even made the game-winning interception in the end zone to secure the win, so you might think I would be ready for my second season at Georgia. But about a month after spring ball, I decided I was headed back home to play football once again for my beloved Southern Methodist University. Oh, yeah, a Mustang once again!

When I returned to Dallas for the summer, I called Forrest Gregg, who had just been named the head football coach at SMU. During our conversation, I asked him to meet with me to discuss returning to SMU and helping him rebuild my favorite SMU Mustangs football program. Everyone thought I had lost my mind, wanting to leave one of the top teams in the country to go back to the weakest team in all of NCAA Division I football. I've always been someone who marches to a different drum than most. I usually follow my heart, and my heart was telling me to follow SMU football and return to my hometown. Once again, I walked on at SMU for a second time and a third time in my career because SMU had already filled all its scholarships for that year. The scholarship didn't bother me much because I was just happy to be home and an SMU Mustang again, and my family could afford the expensive tuition. I redshirted the 1988 season at SMU, which was strategic because we didn't have any games that season due to probation. Since I transferred from Georgia, it was an NCAA requirement that I sit out one year, which meant I was unable to play in games for the 1988 season. That year, our football team only had practice and scrimmages to prepare us for the 1989 season.

The fall of 1989 marked the return of SMU Football, and the whole nation watched with curiosity to see how a team full of freshmen with no college football experience would measure up against a demanding Southwest Conference schedule and a non-conference game against the reigning National Champion Notre Dame Fighting Irish in South Bend. That year, I established myself as a starting slot receiver in a pass-happy run-and-shoot offense, which made me very happy. I also played on all the special teams, returning punts and kickoffs, and was still running down the field on kickoff coverage. We kicked off the season on September 2, 1989, against the Rice Owls. During the 1988 season, with no real games to play, our rallying cry became: 9-2-89! The inaugural game was held at our home stadium, and we lost easily, as we were outmatched in size, speed, and experience, which was evident from the start. Coincidentally, I think not, my daughter was born on this same date, 11 years later. I was one of only four players on our team with previous college football experience. After that first game, our outlook looked grim, and it seemed we faced a demanding and challenging season ahead, to put it mildly.

The next game was scheduled two weeks later, on September 16th, against the University of Connecticut. Coincidentally, I don't think so—my son was born on this same day, 13 years later. During the game, we fell behind early, and by the fourth quarter, we trailed 30-14. Down by 16 points with four minutes remaining, our team, often called the "little engine that could," achieved the impossible, and my name was forever etched in SMU Football history. Known as the "Miracle on Mockingbird" and ranked as the eighth most memorable moment in SMU Football history, we stormed back for a win with no time left on the clock, securing our university and alumni their first victory after the "Death Penalty," with a 31-30 win that quickly became the talk of the nation. It was dubbed the "Miracle on Mockingbird" because the stadium is located on Mockingbird Lane.

Later, a story about this game was written in Sports Illustrated, detailing SMU's historic return to football after the "Death Penalty." Here is a description of the famous play. There are two seconds left on the clock, and our offense is lined up for the last play of the game. The score is 30-25, and we are losing. The stadium is going crazy. Fans who left early and heard the news that we are making a comeback are running across campus and pouring back into the stadium to see what will happen. I was split to the left in the slot as the middle receiver in a three-receiver strong left set. The play was supposed to be a swing pass to our running back, Jason Wolfe, as we had practiced all week. The three receivers were to be decoys, clearing the area for Wolfe to come open in the flat. Our quarterback, Mike Romo, takes the snap and rolls to the left and looks for Wolfe, but immediately the outside linebacker jumps the swing route, so Romo begins to scramble and heads for the end zone in hopes of running the ball in for the score. He moves forward and is met by a couple of defenders. The defensive back, in all the confusion, loses sight of me, and I slip past him into the back of the end zone, and at the last instant, Romo flips the ball to me just as he gets hit, and I make the catch for a touchdown and the win. It was pandemonium!

This is the type of scene where the entire stands empty onto the field and engulfs the players in a sea of out-of-control celebration. After I scored, my whole team stormed the field and met me in the end zone as I raised the ball over my head and my arms in victory. I was lifted up in the air by one of our receivers, Korey Beard, as he was the first of my teammates to arrive. After Korey lifted me, the wave hit us, and we toppled to the ground and were smothered under a pile of bodies, and the bodies just kept coming, wave upon wave. There were so many people raining down on us that it began to get dark, and the only thing I could see was Korey's face and his ear-to-ear grin. I am lying on my back, and Korey is directly on top of me, and we are now face to face as our facemasks are driven into each other because of the weight and mounting pressure of the pile. Now we are being crushed, and I find myself unable to breathe. I tried to catch a breath, but as I exhaled my last breath, the weight of the crowd did not allow me to take any more air into my lungs. I was drowning under a sea of pandemonium, and for a moment, I began to panic. My last words to Korey that I could get out of my mouth were, "I'm dying, I'm dying!" Then I relaxed just before I passed out due to a lack of oxygen and said to myself with a big smile on my face, "What a hell of a way to die!" I thought I was going to die, and in that moment, I was totally okay with my death. I had accepted the most awesome fate I could ever imagine for a football player to die at the bottom of a pile after scoring the game-winning touchdown for the first victory for my beloved SMU after the "Death Penalty!" That would have put a whole new meaning to the term "Death Penalty" in my dark humor!

In reality, at that point in my life, I believed there was no better or more honorable way to die than at the bottom of a pile on a football field, scoring the game-winning touchdown. Thank God, He had different plans because a few minutes later, I woke up to one of my coaches about to give me mouth-to-mouth resuscitation, which I quickly refused and told him to get me the "F#@%" out of here! I was helped off the field and greeted by screaming fans, proud parents and grandparents, and numerous reporters vying for interviews. That night marked one of the biggest celebrations in our school's history, and I was a hero. The next night, I was a live guest on Ted Dawson's Sports Center news program and appeared in newspapers all over the country. I will always be remembered for this famous quote when Ted Dawson asked what it was like after I caught the touchdown pass, and I responded, "It was total jubilation, Ted!" Well it was!

In the 1989 season, we won only one more game, finishing 2-9, but we fought hard, never quit, and established ourselves as one of the toughest and most resilient teams in the country. It was a long and arduous season during which we learned a great deal about ourselves and gained many valuable lessons about perseverance. We faced some painful yet enlightening losses against some of the biggest and best teams in the country: Notre Dame 59-3, Texas 45-13, Baylor 49-3, Texas A&M 63-14, and the worst defeat of the season against the University of Houston 95-21. The last game of the year was against Arkansas, and as a bright spot and a great way to finish the season, we took the lead in the fourth quarter, 24-23, with a few minutes remaining, but couldn't hold on for the victory. The Razorbacks, after beating us, were crowned Southwest Conference Champions and finished 13th in the nation.

For me, the 1989 football season was the most incredible of my life and possibly one of the best years I have ever had. We only won two games, and we faced many matches where we were beaten badly. What I loved most about that year was the way we fought and what we learned about ourselves as young men, which far outweighed any win-loss record, national ranking, or bowl game victory. To me, this exemplified football at its purest—going into a game like David versus Goliath and believing that, despite the odds and the formidable opponent before us, we could somehow dig deep within our hearts and souls to find a victory. We played because we loved the game, and we were grateful that someone gave us a chance to continue playing the sport we loved so much at the next level.

We were a team of undersized overachievers, players whom all the other teams had overlooked and believed could not compete at the college level. We shared this in common, and it made us a feisty, tough, and passionate football team that consistently played as if it were our last game. It was special, and a very special man coached us: Forrest Gregg, a man of faith. Coach Gregg taught us to be warriors and to always believe in ourselves. In football, Forrest Gregg was one of the greatest players to have ever played the game. As a coach, he was among the most outstanding men to lead a team, and as a human being, I have never known anyone finer than him, whom I love dearly. I thank my God for leading me away from Georgia back to SMU. My Lord knew what I needed in football, and it wasn't playing for a national powerhouse that won nearly all its games and was expected to do so. God chose me to return home where my heart had always been, to lead a team against all odds from despair into a fight and a season that was unique and one-of-a-kind, never to be duplicated. There will never again be a college football "Death Penalty," and there will never again be a 1989 SMU football season that laid the foundation for future SMU seasons. This was my dream season, and I was truly blessed beyond measure. At the end of the season, I was given the Wild Mustang Award, presented to the player with the biggest heart and the most spirit, one who encourages his teammates in battle. We had a war cry that I will never forget, inspired by the popular movie "Young

Guns." Whenever we headed onto the field, we would always shout at the top of our lungs, "Regulators, let's ride!" And we did!

The following season was my senior season in 1990, and it was my most productive out of all the seasons in my collegiate career. I was voted team captain and led the team in touchdowns and receptions, earning me Team Offensive Most Valuable Player and Honorable Mention All-Southwest Conference Receiver honors. We had a long and arduous season, and we only won a single game. It was our first game of the season, and out of the gates we smashed Vanderbilt 44-7, a team from the powerful and prestigious Southeastern Conference. I scored three touchdowns in that game and, for the first week of the season, led the nation in scoring. My former coach at the University of Georgia, Vince Dooley, a coaching legend, saw the article and wrote me a very nice handwritten letter congratulating me on my success. I must say, after the previous season and all the butt-whippings, that game felt pretty good. For the rest of the season, we didn't fare so well, losing the next 10 games in a row and finishing the season 1-10, in last place in the Southwest Conference.

My time at SMU as a football player had come to an end, and I was considering a career in professional football. My lifelong dream was to play in the NFL, and I truly believed I had the skills to achieve this goal. After a successful season, I hired a sports agent who started promoting me to the NFL by sending game footage to all the teams. Unfortunately, they all passed me by because of my size, so I had to look elsewhere. Drew Pearson, one of my childhood heroes —a former Super Bowl champion, a three-time All-Pro receiver for the Dallas Cowboys, and now the head coach of the Dallas Texans in the Arena Football League—called me into his office. He offered me a job playing professional arena football. I was honored and thought it was incredible to be offered a position by one of the greatest receivers in the game. Still, I declined and signed a two-year, six-figure contract with the Edmonton Eskimos of the Canadian Football League.

I planned to go to Canada and prove myself there, just like I had everywhere else, and then I could move on to play in the NFL. So, as they say, I packed my bags and headed North. When I say North, I mean almost as far north as you can go before you start heading south! It was so far north that, while I was at training camp, I never saw nighttime; I only saw daylight. The sun only set for a couple of hours each day, and that was called twilight, not darkness. I arrived in Canada not in the best shape because I had been drinking and using drugs more frequently after the football season ended. This had been a pattern in my life for most of it, and the upcoming CFL season had snuck up on me. I had been drinking and using ecstasy and cocaine weekly. I kept telling myself every weekend that this would be the last one and that I would start serious training, but I never followed through. I believe the alcohol and drugs kept me from going to training camp in top shape and cost me my football career. After one week, I was cut by the team, and my contract was terminated. I was released and told to catch the first flight out the next morning. And just like that, it was over! That defeat was more than I could bear, and it hurt me deeply. I was crushed, and deep down, I knew I would never play the game I had loved all my life again, football.

This failure completely knocked the wind out of my sails, and for the first time in my life, I became angry at football, which I had loved deeply. It felt as though she had abandoned me. It was a terrible, unexpected breakup that caught me off guard. I was dumped and then ghosted! She had chosen a new lover, and it wasn't me! This was the first time I had ever gone against my 'never quit, never surrender, never say die' mantra and decided to give up football for good. I was done with it and didn't even try playing elsewhere or in the Arena League, where I had an offer on the table. Football broke my heart! It dumped me like a bad prom date and caused pain I had never felt before. My identity was gone. The notoriety and fame were gone! The intensity of the battle was gone! The pride of being a star athlete was gone! Michael Bowen, the football player, was dead, replaced by a young man diving headfirst into addiction, and the addict was unleashed! After I failed in the CFL, it took me a long time to even attend a football game or watch it on television without feeling sad about what could have been or what once was. It was only when I started coaching my son's youth football teams many years later that I rediscovered the comfort and joy in the game, which had been such a big part of my life and helped shape who

I am today. I also realized I couldn't handle my rage when I didn't have football to channel it on the field. Many times, usually after drinking too much, I would go on destructive sprees where I would break and destroy things—mostly bathrooms in bars I was drinking at or cars in the parking lot—on my way home.

The following excerpt is from a book written by my college football coach, Forrest Gregg. The book is called "Winning in the Trenches" and features a chapter titled "Miracle on Mockingbird," the football play I will always be remembered for. It offers some prophetic insight into what my future after football might look like, based on the young man I was back then, just before addiction took over my life. During my years as a student-athlete, it was "Mustang Reminders" that were used to try to correct my behavior, and later, in my addiction, it was drug rehabilitation programs, mental hospitals, jails, and prisons. The writing was already on the wall back then. Even as a young football player and student-athlete, I was rebellious and prone to trouble.

WINNING IN THE TRENCHES
AUTHOR: FORREST GREGG
PAGE 278, CHAPTER 10

There was one young man on the squad who brought to mind Greg Pruitt. Michael Bowen was a mischievous kid, and like Greg, he broke rules to get me to yell at him. With Michael, it was always something. He would arrive late for team meetings just to agitate me. When my players committed an infraction of some sort, I had a systematic reprimand that I termed "Mustang Reminders." One Mustang Reminder was a series of grass drills up and down the field, with the player stopping every ten yards and performing a drill. Each violation carried a varying sentence. For example, missing class would be four or five Mustang Reminders. I couldn't catch them all the time, but I tried to enlist professors to turn them in. With Bowen, however, I didn't need any assistance; Michael would head out to the field on his own and start doing Mustang Reminders. I think he still owes me a few. ~ **Forrest Gregg**

IV. DEEP IN THE HEART OF TEXAS

PSALM 127:1 (NIV)
Unless the lord builds the house, the builders labor in vain, unless the lord watches over the city, the guards stand watch in vain.

PROVERBS 24:3-4 (NIV)
By wisdom a house is built, and through understanding it is established; through knowledge its rooms are filled with rare and beautiful treasures

MATTHEW 12:25 (NIV)
Every kingdom divided against itself will be ruined, and every city or household divided against itself will not stand

PROVERBS 16:18-19 (KJV)
Pride goeth before destruction, and a haughty spirit before a fall. Better is to be of a humble spirit with the lowly, than to divide the spoil with the proud.

It's just before Christmas in 2009, and the sign on the road says Austin is 14 miles away. Having been away from Texas for 15 years, it felt like "Home Sweet Home" to me, "Deep in the Heart of Texas," the place where I was born and raised, and the sacred ground where I had made a name for myself on the football field. I can already hear my Texas accent returning as I start referring to people as y'all! I am driving a U-Haul with my youngest son and his mother; my brother, sister, and our cat are following behind in another vehicle. The previous day, my dad had picked me up from a prison in Arizona, where I had just finished a 2-year sentence for narcotics sales and felony fleeing and evading when I took the Phoenix Police on a high-speed chase in a stolen car.

Texas marked the start of my new beginning and a chance for redemption. My children's mother, Kara, had divorced me three years earlier because of my ongoing drug addiction and my many "missing-in-action" disappearances, which left her and the kids in a cloud of uncertainty, mistrust, and hopelessness that I would ever overcome my addiction. My inability to stay clean, sober, and out of jail had finally taken its toll. Somehow, Kara decided to give me one more shot, and I was determined to keep my promise to her and the kids that my using days were over. We agreed to reunite the family, pack up all our belongings, and start a new life in a different state and home. My parents also gave me another chance by buying me a new house and a pickup truck. I went to work for my dad in real estate development, with the opportunity to develop some land his family owned in Dallas, Texas. At the time, my parents were living in Austin on Lake Travis, and my twin sister, Missy, lived nearby. When we arrived at our new home in Cedar Park, my parents were there waiting with open arms and excitement. The house was beautiful—more than I had ever imagined when I was sitting locked up in an Arizona prison. I thought to myself, "Michael Bowen, you better not mess this one up!"

I truly believed, like we always do when released from our last incarceration, that my days of abusing alcohol and drugs were behind me. The time in prison I had just served was the event that finally grabbed my attention, and the suffering I endured was enough of a reminder to keep me from ever going back. This was my "major comeback after my minor setback," squandering 20 years of productivity with nothing to show for it but a long line of disappointing events and hurt people along the way. My greatest inspiration at this point was my three amazing children and their mother, who had decided to believe in me one more time, giving me one more chance to finally come through for our family and make good on my promise to lead them and give them a good life where I would be drug-free!

I'm in Texas on parole! I haven't used any drugs in a year and a half, but I still drank alcohol. During my drive from Arizona to Texas, when we stopped and stayed overnight in El Paso, I decided we should celebrate my release with a couple of bottles of wine. That was the first big mistake I made when I bought the wine. I told myself it was just a little wine, and it was, but for someone like me, just a little wine is like a bit of gasoline and a match. This action reopened the door to my addiction and gave me the green light to keep drinking, as I told myself I would only drink socially from now on. That was the seed I planted in my soul with a lie, without thinking about when it would start producing the inevitable, wicked fruit of my addiction. Here we go again!

The second and most damaging mistake was leaving behind my prison Bible and the relationship with God I had started to build when I found what I call "Jailhouse Religion" in Arizona. An experience with Jesus Christ only becomes "Jailhouse Religion" when you leave your relationship with Him in jail and do not bring Him with you when you are released and return to your old ways. At that time, I chose to leave it behind. I again decided to rely on my "own" strength and understanding, and, as my track record shows, I knew what would happen next. I thanked God for freeing me from prison and giving me another chance to reunite with my family, then I said goodbye. I looked at God and received His gift with gratitude. But after accepting His gift, I then looked at the gift and took my eyes off the Giver—that was my final, fatal mistake. You see, I received His blessings and admired the gifts, but I forgot about the Giver. I found myself lost in the gifts, and it happened so quickly! Just like that, I was entirely consumed by the world again, blindly led by my sinful flesh and carnal mind.

Everything was now moving at lightning speed compared to the slow pace of being a prison inmate. Overnight, I went from having zero responsibilities to a whole new set, along with the stresses of rebuilding my life and providing for my family. Looking back now, I threw myself into this new life and acted as if my old life never existed, never addressing the wreckage of the past. I expected my children and their mother to do the same and move forward without considering their unresolved hurts from my past behaviors and abandonment. It was easier for me to focus on this new life and hide my past with the help of new money, a new home, a new career, a new city, and a new hope for a prosperous future. But that was a mistake that would eventually come back to haunt me. I failed to realize that the emotional injuries and damages were still just beneath the surface, brewing like a mighty volcano ready to erupt and destroy everything again. I was unaware that old hurts needed to be resolved and healed. I found myself caught in the fantasy of a new life, believing that it would be the magic wand to fix everything instantly, but it doesn't work like that. I was on a honeymoon of sorts, and we all know honeymoons don't last forever. When something rises, it always falls. All the possessions and experiences that initially excited me would eventually lose their novelty, and that's precisely what happened around the six-month mark of my new life in Deep in the Heart of Texas. The ship that had carried me into my bright future was about to face some severe storms and would soon fall apart, leaving me shipwrecked once more.

My new job in real estate development, working for my dad, was going well. I began building a subdivision in Dallas, Texas, and spent a considerable amount of time traveling between Dallas and Austin. In early 2010, I was contacted by the executive producers making an ESPN 30 for 30 documentary called "Pony-Excess," about my college football team and the NCAA's first-ever "Death Penalty," when they canceled our football program in 1986 for ongoing rules violations and suspended it for two years until it was rebuilt in 1988. Since I played on the 1986 team, as well as the 1989 and 1990 reconstruction teams, after transferring back to SMU following a year at the University of Georgia, the producers wanted to interview me because I had experienced both sides. I was interviewed, and the program aired in December, becoming a huge success. I was featured in the documentary and appeared at the Austin premiere. It was an enjoyable experience and a significant boost to my ego to be recognized again for one of the greatest moments of my life. As Bruce Springsteen sang, "Glory days, well, they'll pass you by, glory days, in the wink of a young girl's eye, glory days, glory days." Well, they certainly did pass me by, but because of this incredible story that became a national sensation in the sports world, they came back to visit one more time, and I loved every minute of it!

That year, I also started coaching my youngest son's football team and rediscovered my love for the game. I was so proud of my son, seeing him fall in love with the game just as I had when I was his age. He was a lot like me on the football field, fearless and tough. I was pumped! One day at practice, during our first season and his first time playing in pads, I was pushing him on the field, and he was lying there whining about something. Mind you, he was only 7 years old then, and I must have hit a nerve because, in the middle of my coaching rant while I was standing over him, he rose to his knees and angrily punched me in the family jewels, dropping me to the ground right at his eye level. The other coaches stared, stunned, unable to believe what they'd just seen. They stood there wondering what I was going to do next. Believe me, I saw red, and my immediate reaction was one of fury. I was shocked as I hit the ground, ready to yell at him when a small voice inside my head said, "Michael, oh boy, you got one!" Instead of yelling, I grabbed his facemask as he was still on the ground, his eyes wide as saucers, probably wondering what he'd just done to his dad. I calmly told him, "I like your fire and your fight, but don't you ever do that to me again!" Woo-Hoo! I didn't know whether to cry or scream from excitement. For a 7-year-old to do that to his dad told me a lot about who he was as a football player and the fight he had in him—a chip off the old block. I was the same way—full of fight—but I could never imagine doing that to my dad. Just thinking about it still scares me today!

This marked the start of a new chapter in my life, where I became fully immersed and dedicated to youth league football and my new identity as "Coach Bo." I coached with passion, teaching the boys how to play and love the game of football, and our team found success. We had three championship seasons in three years and experienced two undefeated seasons, going 21-0 after our first year, losing only two games. We won the city league championship in our first two years and then went on to achieve a regional league title in our third. Our fourth season in 2013 was set to be the first year the boys were old enough to compete for a National Championship and attend games in Florida, including a trip to Disneyland. We believed we had the team that could go all the way! During the third season, I also took on the role of league football commissioner, overseeing operations, which further increased my focus on youth football. I was completely committed, and it became my top priority in life. Looking back now, I realize it was an unhealthy balance in my life!

Youth football is a lot of fun for us parents, especially when the team is competitive and winning championships. I poured my heart and soul into our team and the boys. My main goal was to create an experience for them and their families that they would remember for a lifetime—an unforgettable experience. My heartfelt wish for the boys was for them to learn to believe in themselves as winners and to fall in love with the game, just as I did when I was 10. I dedicated myself entirely to building a winning team and creating a memorable experience, to the point that it started negatively affecting other parts of my life. During football season, everything else was put on hold, and my relationships and business suffered as a result. When it came to football, all I knew was that if you gave it your all, you could succeed. I lived by the saying, "Hard work beats talent when talent fails to work." I learned this from my college football coach, Forrest Gregg, who learned it from his coach, Vince Lombardi, whom I proudly called my grand-coach! My belief has always been to work hard, stay tough, always play to win, and never give up! Coach Gregg instilled this into our 1989 SMU Mustang football team, as he was later quoted as saying, "And they took this lesson to the gospel!" I can say the same about our boys who won those championships. Those kids were something else!

During this time, my daughter competed in cheerleading in the same league as our football team. Her cheer team was one of the best in the league, earning them a trip to the National Championships at

Disneyland in Florida, where they finished 5th in the country. Our family was very involved in youth sports, and the kids seemed happy, surrounded by a large group of friends. I made a mistake then by not focusing enough on their schoolwork and putting sports before academics. I regret this and believe it hurt my children and taught them the wrong priorities in life. I taught them that sports came first and everything else, including God, was secondary, because I wasn't taking them to church or teaching them about who created them, loved them, and wanted a relationship with them through His son Jesus Christ. I knew better. No excuse!

Over the three years leading up to 2012, my relationship with my children's mother became deeply fractured as I continued drinking heavily and struggled to manage other parts of my life effectively. I was selfishly absorbed by youth football and the pressure of working out of town in Dallas, and things began to decline. I had finished building a subdivision and was planning my next project, which was to develop a retail center adjacent to the subdivision. This center was to be owned by my parents and sisters. My lack of focus, increased drinking, and occasional drug use started to damage my plans, and they began to fall apart. I was drinking every day and had a few incidents where I went missing for several days, smoking crack. The warning signs were clear, and my family members sensed what was coming. No matter how tightly I tried to hold onto my life, my record indicated a very destructive future.

Another difficult moment that year was when my cousin Scott was diagnosed with pancreatic cancer. He was my hero growing up, and although we drifted apart as adults, we reconnected a couple of years before he got sick. He started coming to football games and supporting my kids. He was so good with them, and they grew to love him. When we found out Scott had cancer, we kept our hopes and prayers alive, but in February 2013, on Valentine's Day, he passed away. Before he died, he made peace with Jesus and gave his life to Him. Praise the Lord, my cousin was saved and now has eternal life in the Kingdom of Heaven.

Not realizing it at the time, I took it extremely hard in retrospect. Two days before he passed, I took my children to Dallas to say our goodbyes to Scott, as he called me and said he didn't have much longer to live. When we saw him, it shook us to the core. Scott was a big giant of a man—like a big old teddy bear with a million-dollar smile, and now he was just a shell of what he once was. He had deteriorated and lost so much weight. As soon as we saw him in the hospital, we all began to cry. Scott, on the other hand, just smiled his big smile, and I could see a sparkle in his eyes. I was a wreck at this point. The night before, I had been drinking all night and had visited the crack house to self-medicate my feelings, knowing I was about to see my cousin for the last time. I was on zero sleep, still a bit under the influence, and unable to properly say my goodbyes or pray with Scott and the family.

Two weeks after Scott's death, I went to a bar to take the edge off with some moderate drinking, planning to be home at a decent hour because my kids were waiting at home, and I was responsible for waking them up, making breakfast, and driving them to school. Throughout the night, I talked and texted several friends as I usually do when drinking, trying to get them to join me, but nobody could that night. As the hours passed, I abandoned my plan of moderation and became completely intoxicated, stumbling drunk. When the bars closed, instead of going home, I decided to drive around looking for something much stronger than alcohol. In a nearly blackout state, I searched for the knockout punch of a crack cocaine high! I eventually found what I was looking for, but I never made it home. That night, I ran away from my life, abandoning my children and all my responsibilities. I disappeared into thin air, vanishing without a trace, just as I had done so many times before! What a loser. What a selfish man. How could anyone do something so terrible? How could I fall into that pit again? Back into the darkness I go, and only Jesus knows where I will end up!

V. CAPTURED BY GOD

2 TIMOTHY 2:20-26 (ESV)

Now, in a great house, there are not only vessels of gold and silver but also of wood and clay, some for honorable use, some for dishonorable. Therefore, if anyone cleanses himself from what is dishonorable, he will be a vessel for honorable use, set apart as holy, useful to the master of the house, ready for every good work. So, flee youthful passions and pursue righteousness, faith, love, and peace, along with those who call on the lord from a pure heart. Have nothing to do with foolish, ignorant controversies; you know that they breed quarrels. And the lord's servant must not be quarrelsome but kind to everyone, able to teach, patiently enduring evil, correcting his opponents with gentleness. God may perhaps grant them repentance leading to a knowledge of the truth, and they may come to their senses and escape from the snare of the devil, after being captured by him to do his will.

Once again, I fell through the cracked windowpane of my addiction and believed the lie that I could drink alcohol like a normal person, smoke a little crack, and then go home as if nothing had happened. This lie has haunted me my whole life, causing me so much pain and disappointment, and devastating many of my loved ones! It sent me crashing into the dark world of crack cocaine once more. You would think I'd have enough sense by now to recognize the warning signs and stop the inevitable, but no, not me! I had disappeared from my life, my children, my friends, my loved ones, and all my responsibilities, trading them in for a life under the influence of alcohol, crack cocaine, and methamphetamine. I wanted to get high more than I wanted to live life. I was running wild through the streets of Austin, Texas, feeding my addiction, with alcohol and drugs screaming for more. I didn't realize at the time that I was under spiritual attack and that the devil was coming for my soul. I was convinced I had fallen so far and done something so terrible that I could never return to the life I had left behind. I was paralyzed by fear, and this lie had cut me off from any positive thoughts that could have helped me regain my senses and remember that my family, my children, and my friends love me and want me to come home. In the grip of my addiction, I couldn't think of the good things in my life that might help pull me out of darkness and back to those who love me. This is the captivity where I am chained to the craving for more drugs and higher highs, feeding the demons of my addiction. These demons are feeding on the light of my soul, trying to extinguish it, pushing me deeper and deeper into a rathole—the horrible pit of my addicted life.

The money I had when I left the house that night is gone, and I have emptied my bank account. I have nothing left to buy drugs with, so I am forced to steal from others while driving around Austin in my Lexus, shoplifting from many stores that have become targets of my addictive mind. Just the fact that I was shoplifting in a Lexus is madness enough and a testament to this crazy, absurd life my addiction has led me into. I couldn't even put $10 worth of gas into my car. I had to steal from people and businesses to pay for gas and the illegal street drugs I can't stop using. This is the vicious cycle of addiction that shows no mercy. Addiction wants only one thing: once you surrender and bow to it, everything that can be stolen, sold, or traded to keep the sickness alive becomes fair game. This is the ugliness of addiction and its mockery of the once productive life the addict had.

One day, I was shoplifting and ran out of a store with a home theater system under my arm as the alarm blared. One of the store's employees was chasing me, right on my heels. I jumped into my Lexus, tossing the home theater system into the back, and as I did, the key fell beneath the passenger seat. The store employee reached my vehicle just as I managed to lock the doors. I frantically looked for the key under the seat while he jumped on the hood, threatening me with a fist and some choice words. I finally found the key, started the engine, and shot back some choice words and a rude hand gesture. He grabbed my windshield wiper, bent it back, and angrily jumped to the ground as I sped off, heading for the parking lot exit. I drove away with my loot and the cash to feed my addiction. The dope man is going to love this item.

Looking back now, I realize that if I had been at that store a few months earlier—before I fell apart and got lost again in my addiction—and had seen someone doing what I was doing now, I probably would have chased that person down and tried to stop them. I would have thought, 'What a loser,' 'What a scumbag,' 'What a lowlife!' That's how far I had fallen. I had become a completely different person inside the drugs, someone who would have disgusted me just a few months earlier. Self-hatred was growing inside me about who I had turned into. On top of that, what kind of role model was I to my children and to all the boys I coached in football and track? Those boys loved Coach Bo and thought I was amazing! That torment was also in my mind, as I was out there doing such terrible things. I believe the shame and guilt of those thoughts only added fuel to the fire that kept me trapped in my addiction and driven by the insatiable craving for more drugs.

After several months of smoking crack daily and using methamphetamine, I walked into the bathroom at a crack house where I was smoking drugs. As I entered and shut the door behind me, I looked in the mirror, and it scared me to death because I had no idea who was looking back at me. It startled me because I thought a stranger was in there with me. I cautiously looked in the mirror, unsure of what I was seeing, and realized that I was the stranger looking back at me, and I didn't even recognize myself. All I saw was a stranger with darkness in his eyes. I knew I had lost myself and become something completely different from what I had ever been. I hated that man in the mirror. He was one scary dude! After a moment, I looked away and couldn't bring myself to look back into the mirror again. I wrote a poem about this experience, titled "MIRRORS," which you can read at the end of this book.

At my lowest point, I was living out of my car, smoking crack, selling crack, doing meth, driving from one drug house to another in search of drugs, and committing theft after theft to feed my disgusting habit. One day, while I was driving on my drug-fueled quest for more, a song about Jesus came on the radio. As I listened, my soul began to ache, and I felt a deep sense of conflict. I screamed, "I can't listen to this anymore!" and switched the radio station to something else. I had just rejected the one who was coming to help me. I believe that God said right then, "THAT'S IT. ENOUGH IS ENOUGH." I think this because just a few hours later, I was pulled over by the Austin police for six outstanding felony warrants for theft. That was Sunday, May 19, 2013. This is the day I now call the day I was "Captured by God."

You know you've fallen a long way when you're sitting in the back of a police car, thankful you're on your way to jail, and finally, the nightmare is over. The police that Sunday night saved me from destruction and pulled me out of danger into safety. They helped me stop using drugs by locking me up in jail, away from their wicked grasp. I had fallen so far, now with a methamphetamine addiction added to my crack cocaine addiction, and this meth addiction made crack seem like child's play. Satan had set a new hook in my flesh that made the hook of crack look small. Meth took me to a place I had never been before with drugs, into the world of injecting drugs into my veins. My new "hook-up" for meth, after knowing him for two days, gave me a bag of syringes. I asked him what they were for because I didn't shoot drugs into my veins, and he said, "Just hold on to them, you will need them one day." That was a cold, hard statement! But he was right. The first day I bought meth from him, I snorted it. The second day, I bought a pipe and started smoking it, and on the third day, I pulled a syringe and began shooting it into my veins. After 25 years, I had only faced the monster meth on occasion, but now, the enemy was using it as my final death blow. In this new world, I quickly fell into the deepest, darkest rat hole of my entire life. But only by the grace of God and His mercy, on that Sunday, May 19, 2013, my sweet Jesus reached His loving hand into the filthy pit of crack cocaine and methamphetamine addiction and pulled me out, saying, "No More!"

God snatched me up unexpectedly, finally answering my cry for help that I had shouted a few weeks earlier when I was in that crack house and yelled, "Stooooooooooooooopppppp." God took me by the hand and placed me in a cell at the downtown Travis County Jail. I was a complete wreck, like a door kicked off its hinges, broken and used for firewood. I had lost about 25 pounds; my arms were torn up from needles, and my hair and beard were unkempt. My eyes were as dark as coal, and who knows how many unclean spirits had taken over my soul. I looked terrible. I went to my cell, climbed onto my bunk, and fell asleep. Those of us who have been addicted to drugs know all too well what that feels like. When you lie down on your bunk, knowing you'll be there for a while, and you're not even upset about it, but relieved that you're finally out in the chaos of the streets, addicted to drugs. Thank you, Jesus! That first night in jail, I fell into the deepest sleep I've had in months.

During my time on the streets, I sometimes went without sleep for up to seven or eight consecutive days. During that period, I ate and drank very little. It was smoke, smoke, and more smoke, and I shot drugs into my veins around the clock, robbing and stealing from people to keep getting high. After a run like that, my body was about to give out, and I needed to lie down and rest, which usually allowed me to recover. That was my condition when I hit Tavis County Jail. I spent three days downtown before being moved to the central jail in Del Valle, Texas, to wait for my court appearance on multiple felony theft charges.

After a few weeks in Del Valle, one of my good friends and fellow coaches of our youth football team, Matt Hoenig, came to visit me and asked what had happened to me and where I had been. I gave him a brief outline of the story, and he told me that he and our friends had been worried and searching for me. He encouraged me and helped me reconnect with reality and my old life. During our conversation, an interesting incident occurred. As I was talking to Matt, I asked him if he had spoken to my parents because I had been writing to them, and they had not written back, nor were they accepting my calls from jail. They were tired of my drug addiction, and I do not blame them one bit. Matt told me that yes, he had spoken to them. I asked him how they were doing, and he said they were doing well. Then Matt asked me if I knew they had moved, and I told him no. I asked him where they had moved, and he told me that my mom and dad said not to tell me. I was in shock. My parents moved, and they didn't want me to know where they were living. When our conversation was over, I made the walk back to my cell, and I couldn't shake the disappointment and hurt that were welling up inside me. I began to feel like they had abandoned me—and even worse, I felt like they had rejected and disowned me. When I got to my cell, I climbed into my bed and pulled the covers over my head because I felt like I was going to cry. In jail, you do not want to let people see you cry, or they will think you are weak, and that is not good.

 I am in my bed with the covers over my head, and I began crying and having a big old pity party. Waah, waah, crying like a baby boy! I was saying to God over and over, my mother has abandoned me, and my parents have disowned me. Waah, Waah, Waah! I was feeling sorry for myself, hoping God would comfort me. And then I heard these thundering words, "STOP IT, THEY AREN'T YOUR SAVIOR, I AM!" When I heard Him say this, I shut up immediately. When God speaks to you, it settles it. At that moment, I stopped crying and realized that this was the truth. For so many years, I would count on my parents to bail me out and save me from all the problems I brought upon myself because of my addiction. And out of their love for me, they would always come to my rescue and save me. That was not fair to them. They were being held hostage by their love for me, and that was not right. God was telling me the truth when He said He was my Savior, and I should never look anywhere else. Thank you, Jesus, for revealing this truth to me!

 That visit reconnected me to a part of myself I thought I had lost forever. The love and support of my friend that day is something

I will treasure forever. That gave me my first positive thought in months: maybe I had what it took for another comeback. I am also grateful that the Lord told me He would save me this time around! I was in jail now and knew I would be there for a long time. Over the next several months, other friends reached out with letters of encouragement, telling me they still believed in me. Gary and Marsha Johnston, Nate and Caterria Anderson, Kevin and Linda Adams, and Kimberly Hutchinson, your words during my darkest days were a light! Thank you!

Behind bars, my addiction still raged in my body and mind, and I was under spiritual attack. The enemy believed he would soon destroy me or steal my soul, but God had other plans. Jail is both an addict's blessing and curse. It's a blessing because we're safe from the drugs that could kill us, and a curse because we can't reach the drugs we crave. It's a place of terrible conflict—of body, soul, and spirit. Take the worst addicts off the streets during the height of their addiction, remove their drugs, and lock them all together in a cage where everyone is angry and forced to face the wreckage they've caused. Add in those with mental illness and others who hate obeying the law, and that's the county jail. It's a time of chaos, as the entire place feels like it could blow at any second. One wrong word or misstep, and fists and fury erupt everywhere!

After a few weeks, I settled into my new home. Once I finally acclimated to my surroundings and found my place in the pod, I began to relax a little. Just when I thought I was finally going to be able to unwind, my mind erupted into chaos, and I started to experience wave after wave of relentless, back-and-forth thoughts. These thoughts started pounding on me, trying to pull me into facing my life and the wreckage I had caused during my three months of wildness, lost in the darkness of my addicted hell, chained to drugs and alcohol. The waves began slowly, but day after day, they grew stronger and pushed against me like a storm building on the ocean, crashing against the rocky coast in a relentless surge. I fought back and resisted, keeping my defenses up to guard against emotions that were about to explode. I knew that if I cracked even a little, I might shatter into a million pieces and never stop crying. I was overwhelmed with sadness inside! I felt consumed by guilt and shame! I was emotionally devastated and afraid of what lay behind the wall I had built so securely, which I was desperately trying not to tear down. I wasn't ready to face my reality! I didn't think I could handle the pain and disappointment lurking behind that concrete wall. I held firm and put up a strong front to avoid completely losing control, but the pressure kept mounting and finally became more than I could bear.

I developed the habit of walking laps around the day room in the dorm to stay active, which helped prevent the weight of my situation from overwhelming me. One night, as I turned the corner near the dip and chin-up bars, the dorm started to feel different. A terrible blanket of darkness suddenly covered me, and for a moment, I believed I was back in hell, just like that time in the crack house when I thought I had died. At that point, everything seemed to scream that I was in hell with no way out. It was just like before, and I was overcome with torment and grief again. However, this time it didn't last long, and I quickly walked to my bed, knelt down, and began to pray, pulling me back into reality. But this time, I also felt a desire to stop running from myself and an intense hunger to read the Word of God. I can only describe this feeling as a whirlwind inside my soul—blowing and swirling so fiercely it almost twisted my body. It shook and tore apart everything inside me. So much was happening internally, and when it stopped, I had an overwhelming urge to pick up the Bible and read. I grabbed a Bible and started reading God's Word, unable to put it down. I think I read the New Testament in a week, then began on the Old Testament, switching back to the New at times. I couldn't get enough! Through reading God's Word, I felt my soul begin to heal. I started praying to Jesus nonstop, talking with Him day and night. Now, my walks around the dorm's day room became constant conversations with the lover of my soul, my rescuer, and my redeemer. God began to consume me, and I just wanted more. I cried myself to sleep, softly sang worship songs, and praised the Lord right there on my bottom bunk in Dorm 1-G, cell fourteen, in Travis County Jail.

After spending a few months in county jail, it was finally my turn to appear before the judge for my charges. Four of the six felony theft charges were dropped, and I pleaded guilty to the remaining two. During my first court appearance, I was there with my court-appointed attorney, and I pleaded guilty to the charges. I was then told to return in two weeks for sentencing. About a week later, I received a visit from my attorney, who informed me that they would be offering me probation and that I would be released from prison. I was ecstatic and began planning my release. After two months in jail, I still felt shaky and sensed some lingering addiction. I felt pretty confident because I had been reading the Word and starting to heal, but I was still far from being truly free. I planned to move in with a friend until I could get back on my feet, and I intended to get involved with a church and work toward a new life free from drugs and alcohol. At the time, I thought the probation I was given was a blessing from God. Man, was I wrong about that!

Two weeks had passed, and I went to court again, expecting to be released after that day's proceedings. I knew something was wrong when I first looked at my attorney, who had called me out of the holding cell into a smaller interview room. I could tell by her expression that something was wrong, and when she delivered the news, my heart sank, and I felt so disappointed. The judge had thoroughly reviewed my file and saw that, in my past, I had never completed any probation and had always absconded, going on the run. My attorney told me they were going to give me a one-year sentence at Travis State Jail. She asked if I wanted her to try to get it reduced to six months, and I told her no. I explained I had already told the Lord that whatever happens at court that day, I would accept it, believing it was from Him, so I decided to sign for the year.

After sentencing, I returned to the county jail to wait for my transfer to prison. As soon as I got back to my cell, I went to my bunk, kneeled in prayer, and searched my heart and mind for a heartfelt prayer. All I could think of was, "I hate myself. I hate myself. I hate myself." I kept searching for more words, but still, all that came out was, 'I hate myself. I hate myself. I hate myself." Eventually, I reached a point where I hated the person I had become. That's when God said to me, "GOOD, I CAN WORK WITH THAT." You see, I had to reach a point where I hated myself enough to let the "Old Man" inside of me and open the way for God to make me a new creation. That's when I started my breakthrough, and I understood why God made me go to prison for a year. He wasn't finished with me yet. If I had gotten out on probation, I wouldn't have been able to make it. I wasn't where the Lord needed me to be in Him. Thank you, Jesus, for always knowing what is best, even when I can't see it myself.

After another week or so, I was transferred to prison. When I arrived, they stripped me down butt naked, made me bend over and cough, and shaved my head. They then gave me a bedroll, some linens, clothes, and a towel, along with a bar of soap, a toothbrush, and some toothpaste, and sent me to the caged area at the Travis Unit. The cages are a place you go for the first week of your incarceration, where they lock you and about eleven others in a cage while they process you and determine what dorm they will send you to for your housing assignment. This was my second time in prison, so I was familiar with the process.

After my week in the cages, I was transferred to a dorm where they had a drug and alcohol rehabilitation program called Turning Points. As soon as I arrived, I placed my belongings on the top bunk, and my new "Cellie," Willie Frazer, asked me if I was a Wood, which is a Caucasian prison gang, and I said no, "I am down with Jesus Christ!" He said that he, too, was down with JC! God is good and had me in the right place. I was already being blessed. That first night, they called for Chapel, and I went. I was walking down the hall, about to enter the Chapel, and the Lord spoke to me, telling me this was why He had me here in prison: to learn about who He was and to enter into a relationship with Him through Jesus Christ. I began to cry as I walked through the door, and soon I started worshiping and praising

Him. That first night at the service, I was weeping and crying, saying over and over, "Jesus, where are you?" After repeating this several times, I heard the Lord whisper to me, "I'M IN YOUR TEARS, MICHAEL." That just wrecked me, but also anchored deep into my spirit the truth that Jesus is in my sadness and sorrow. He has been with me through it all!

ISAIAH 53:4 (NKJV)

Surely He has borne our griefs and carried our sorrows; yet we esteemed Him stricken, smitten by God, and afflicted.

My worship was pure and heartfelt, and I was calling on the name of Jesus Christ, who had just rescued me from a dark, drug-addicted pit. He saved me from losing my soul to the devil when the devil came to me in a crack house and offered to get me out of the mess I was in and give me power over the drugs if I would give him my soul in return. Jesus saved me from the eternal torment of hell, where there is constant weeping and gnashing of teeth. I had finally found my God.

About six weeks later, I was at a Thursday night service during praise and worship when I fell to my knees in surrender. It was during a song by Jason Upton called "A Better Way," and as I listened, I was brought to my knees, begging Jesus to save me. I was crying uncontrollably, with snot pouring out of my nose. I wept with godly sorrow, asking God to forgive me of my sins. I kept repeating, "I hate myself. I hate this world. I don't want it anymore. Please forgive me for all the wicked things I have done. All I want is You, Jesus." I told Jesus, "You know my future, and if I am going to leave this prison and go back to smoking crack, then just go ahead and kill me now because I can't live another day like this." Then I said, "But if you save me, I will serve you the rest of the days of my life!" Suddenly, I felt the hand of God come down on me like a hammer on my head, and I felt my soul crack, my spirit beginning to pour out onto the floor like dirty, filthy water. I wept on that floor, pleading with Jesus to rescue me, tears streaming down my face, snot pouring from my nose. Just as I felt myself almost empty, I felt my addiction leave my body, and I began to shake. I didn't know what to do next. That thing that had been a part of me for so long was now gone. I was on my knees on the prison chapel floor, shaking, not knowing what to do next. Then I heard God say, "STAND UP, MY SON!" I stood, feeling His presence, and a peace that surpasses all understanding swept over me. I knew in that moment I was changed—that He had heard my cry. My whole life transformed in an instant. I believe that when I surrendered my life to Him and committed to serving Him for the rest of my days after repenting with godly sorrow, His truth set me free, and He made me His own. That day, Evangelist Michael Bowen stepped out of darkness into the Light of Jesus Christ, and I was born again! I chose to follow Jesus and become His disciple, with no turning back.

A few weeks after that chapel service, I was sitting at a table in the dorm when a younger brother approached me and asked, "Coach, how do you know when the Holy Spirit is here?" I was called Coach because I coached youth football and often talked about it, so that's what they called me. If anyone wanted to speak to Coach, they would be talking about Jesus because Coach was all about Jesus. I answered him with an analogy: it's like the wind. As I shared, I heard a voice speak to my spirit, saying, "Why don't you invite me to the table?" I immediately stopped and began to pray. As I prayed for Jesus to come to the table with us, the Holy Spirit invaded us, and we found ourselves in the presence of Almighty God. All we could do was stare at each other, breathless. I will never forget this moment because it was the day I was filled with the Holy Spirit—power, fire, and an unending love beyond words. This was the day the Lord had made, and I will rejoice and be glad in it. This is the day I received the baptism of the Holy Ghost. That day, I began praying in tongues and gained new revelations and insights about my life. I even wrote a poem about this experience called "FACE TO FACE," which you can read at the end of this chapter.

During my time in prison, I attended every church service I could. I also participated in Christian-based classes and absorbed all the information they provided. The volunteers who came into the prison touched my life and encouraged me that I could succeed once I was released. I loved my weekly evening Bible studies and worship sessions with Ron and Katie Brigmon. One thing I appreciated about their services was that they treated me like a normal human being. While I was with them, I didn't feel like a prison inmate. I still have a great relationship with them today. Sonny Kitchen taught another class I loved. He was a man who found great success after he was released from prison, having given his life to Jesus. He came back to share his story with us and teach us valuable skills that we would need to be successful when we are released back into society. I owe a debt of gratitude to all the prison ministers who shared their love, strength, and hope in Jesus Christ with me. Whenever they entered the prison, I saw a light in them that I wanted to have in myself. That was all part of God's plan to bring me into that prison and show me the light in them that He wanted to give to me. That light led me to surrender.

My hope for you, as you read this book and if you are incarcerated, is that you do not see your situation as a negative thing. The worst day of your life isn't the first day you found yourself in jail or prison. That day isn't the worst. The worst day is the day before you went to jail or prison. Remember that day now, and say amen if you agree! If you had spent another day out in the world, on those streets, you might have died in your sins, and you would be in hell. But God loved you so much that He had you arrested. He captured you so He could do a good work in you. Now that you are captured, it's time to surrender and accept this God-ordained discipline and chastisement. This discipline is meant for your good and to help you be set free, just like I was. Embrace it now!

HEBREWS 4:12-6 (NIV)

In your struggle against sin, you have not yet resisted to the point of shedding your blood. And have you completely forgotten this word of encouragement that addresses you as a father addresses his son? It says, "my son, do not make light of the lord's discipline, and do not lose heart when he rebukes you, because the lord disciplines the one, he loves, and he chastens everyone he accepts as his son."

God moved within me in a way I had never experienced before. My life had been shattered, my soul tormented, my spirit broken, and my mind ravaged. My sweet Jesus entered my despair, reached into the depths of my darkness, took my hand, and saved me from myself and the enemies of my soul. Praise Jesus, my Creator, King of the Universe, King of Kings, who has power and authority over everything in Heaven and in this fallen world we call Earth. God revealed the truth in Jesus Christ and showed me that I was predestined as His chosen child to serve Him and never again serve the world, my flesh, the devil, or his wicked idols of alcohol and drugs. This prison was where God rebuilt me and made me the man of God that He created me to be. This was my ground zero! The old saying goes, "Let Go and Let God," and I did just that—let go of everything I had ever tried to hold onto in my life. I gave everything to God and left nothing outside of His control.

There is a wall in Tucson, Arizona, on 22nd Street that I always drove past, and it had writing on it that said, "Happiness Is Submission to God." Now I understand exactly what that sign means. I finally had to admit to myself that I was unprepared and unable to manage my own life, and that my best thinking and most significant efforts always led me to addiction, jail, and prison. In this acknowledgment, I found freedom—freeing myself from dependence on myself and the world to bring me happiness. Now I can entrust everything into God's hands and submit to His will instead of my own. His way is much better than mine! I decided to submit and surrender to Him and His "Better Way".

The Lord has poured out His amazing grace, love, and acceptance on me. This is what keeps me surrendered to Him each new day. I've discovered that this is the love I've always searched for but could never find. It's the love I've chased my whole life, and it always escaped me until I surrendered to God's love, which is the truth revealed in Jesus Christ. His love is pure and extraordinary, replacing everything I once relied on for happiness that ultimately let me down. Jesus Christ, who is God made flesh, created the universe and now governs my life. God's Spirit dwells within me. I am His cherished child, reborn through the Spirit, and I will see the Kingdom of Heaven. God didn't create me to be an underachiever, a failure, or to worship worthless idols. He didn't make me a drug addict or a convict. And He certainly never intended for me to live defeated. God has shown me through Jesus Christ that I am victorious in Him—that I am His child. He also revealed the truth about my addiction, which is just the same old lie Satan told Adam and Eve in the garden—that I can overcome it by believing and accepting Him as my Lord and Savior.

While participating in the Turning Points rehabilitation program, my counselor, Ms. Francesca Bridges, assigned me several tasks to help me connect with myself and my faith. She is a Christian, and we often discussed Jesus at length. One day, she asked me to write a paragraph about which animal I would be if I could choose. I thought about it and decided to write it later that evening, just before going to bed, in my bunk. I always kept a notebook with me for journaling and noting my thoughts and reflections on God. That afternoon, during a profound and fiery revelation, as I walked down the outdoor corridor of the Travis Unit along a long walkway called the "Bowling Alley," the idea of "Thunder Horse" was born.

Thunder Horse is my response to the question Ms. Bridges gave to me when she asked me, "If you were an animal, what animal would you be?" While walking down the "Bowling Alley", God began speaking to me. He told me I was a horse. I was not only a horse; I was His horse, and I was a War Horse. His War Horse! After he spoke that Word to me and after I made it through the "Bowling Alley" to the main building, I got caught in the prisoner head count and had to sit in a chair in the hallway until the count was cleared. I wrote a short story named "THUNDER HORSE" as a revelation from God when He gave me my new name and my new charge! You can read this powerful Word from God at the end of this chapter. I AM Thunder Horse!

Shortly after writing Thunder Horse, I was inspired to start this book. Through the Holy Spirit, revelation began flowing into my heart. From my heart, my pen began recording in my journals the truth about my addiction and my identity as a child of God in Jesus Christ. The truth is that I was created for a purpose, and now, as a disciple, I must live out my purpose in faith and obedience. Most of the poetry in this book was written over the next several months after God gave me the revelation of Thunder Horse. The majority of the book was scribbled in my journals and on scraps of paper I collected while I was incarcerated. By then, I had moved to a different dorm and had a new "Cellie," Joshua Culp. Josh can tell you today about all the things I was writing in my journals back then. He can also attest that what I wrote was prophetic, as he witnessed me write it and has seen the things I shared with him come to pass. The Holy Spirit guided all of this through revelation. I prayed to Jesus for Him to make this book His own, or maybe He told me that this book belongs to Him. Either way, here it is for you to read, and you are already a little over halfway through.

This book came to life when I was born again and started working out my salvation with fear and trembling. It was written for the drug addict and prisoner who still lives in defeat. Its purpose is so they can gain the knowledge, wisdom, and understanding through the witness of my journey and testimony, that they too can overcome their addictions and habitual incarcerations by surrendering their lives to Jesus Christ and becoming His disciple, just as I have done. There is no addiction in Jesus Christ, and victory is available to all who surrender their lives to Him.

This book is not just for people battling addiction; it is also for anyone who wants to draw closer to God through Jesus Christ and, most importantly, for those seeking the truth about God and His plan of salvation. If you haven't asked Jesus into your heart and surrendered your life to Him, believing in Him and His name, I encourage you to do so now. You are that one!

1 TIMOTHY 2:3-4 (NKJV)

For this is good and acceptable in the sight of God our Savior, who desires all men to be saved and to come to the knowledge of the truth.

MATTHEW 18:11-14 (NKJV)

For the Son of Man has come to save that which was lost. "What do you think? If a man has a hundred sheep, and one of them goes astray, does he not leave the ninety-nine and go to the mountains to seek the one that is straying? And if he should find it, assuredly, I say to you, he rejoices more over that sheep than over the ninety-nine that did not go astray. Even so it is not the will of your Father who is in heaven that one of these little ones should perish.

JOHN 1:12-13 (NKJV)

But as many as received Him, to them He gave the right to become children of God, to those who believe in His name: who were born, not of blood, nor of the will of the flesh, nor of the will of man, but of God.

While I was in prison, going through the process of letting the old addicted man in me die so I could become a new creation in Jesus Christ, He placed the desire in my heart to start a ministry called Sons & Daughters of Thunder. Sons & Daughters of Thunder are men and women dedicated to helping others come to the knowledge and understanding that only Jesus can deliver us from loneliness, brokenness, hurt, misery, and pain when we surrender our lives to Him, repent of our sins, and allow Him to live in our hearts through the indwelling of the Holy Spirit. We are delivered from the captivity, darkness, and hell of addiction and are called to become His disciples, serving Him for the rest of the days of our lives. In 2013, I spent Christmas in prison, and it was the greatest Christmas I have ever had because this CHRISTmas, I finally received the greatest gift of my life: Jesus Christ.

Jesus also gave me the blueprint for a Christian Drug Rehabilitation Discipleship Program called Thunder House for people who are addicted to drugs or have been in prison. This program provides men and women who wish to become Disciples of Jesus Christ with a place to live in a peaceful environment, a secure home, and a quiet resting place—a sanctuary.

ISAIAH 32:18 (NKJV)
My people will dwell in a peaceful habitation, in secure dwellings, and in quiet resting places

Thunder House is a place where people can go to be set free from drug addiction and discover a "Better Way" of living. It is a place where they can learn to live Christ-centered, Spirit-filled lives and become Sons and Daughters of Thunder. This is now my mission—to help others as I have been helped and to show others the way out of addiction and habitual incarceration once and for all. This is my new life in Jesus Christ, my purpose, and my calling. Through this, I have finally found my true identity in Him and peace for my soul. In this, I have found true success! I was finally released from prison on May 27, 2014, when God opened the gate and said to me, "THUNDER HORSE…LET'S RIDE!"

THUNDER HORSE

I am a fiery, wild horse charging furiously alone across a high desert plateau; my home. It is a brisk fall day, and a cold nip is in the air. Breath, like billowing smoke, is pouring from my snorting nostrils as I eat up the ground in defiant rebellion. There is a mighty storm on the horizon brewing from the North as dark clouds accented with lightning and thunder begin to fill the once calm air.

I can feel the rolling thunder and the power emanating from the storm that is filling every part of my being. I am full of fear and excitement, the two things that I love the most, yet I cannot understand their meaning, so I do what I was created to do, which is to run! Run fast, run hard, pound the earth, and eat up the ground with an uncertain vengeance. This plateau is mine. I own it and everything in it! This is where I thrive and where I have been made, wrought out of the dirt and the cold, brisk air that make up my powerful body and unbridled spirit.

The storm continues its onward approach, moving dreadfully across the plateau like a mighty advancing army kicking up dust as if it were coming specifically for me. Not knowing why and against all sound reason, I turn, size up the storm, and I charge! My hooves pounding, every muscle in my body responding to its call; I dig deep into the hardened earth, tearing up the sacred ground, and I am swallowed up in the midst of the storm's awesome presence.

At once! A flash of white-hot, blinding lightning presents itself to me, followed by a loud crash of booming thunder. In an instant, I am stopped dead in my tracks in glorious fear. I rise to my powerful hind legs and paw frantically at the unsuspecting air. What is this? I ask myself in frenzied wonder. It feels like a part of me. I recognize its strength, yet I still can't fully comprehend its meaning. Another flash, another roar of thunder, and I am settled back to the ground as I face off with the magnificent storm in a curious, fearful stare. A snort, a shake of my forceful head, a paw at the unyielding ground; I struggle to take in its awesome splendor with all of my wild senses. I am drawn to it in amazement and succumb to it by fear. In power and overwhelming majesty, it wraps itself around me like a whirlwind as it moves through my soul, stirring every part of my inner being.

At first, I struggle and strain as I feel it trying to bring me under its control. I fight for a moment in vain, and then slowly I yield to its striking power as it begins to comfort me and speak to me with its still, soft, awe-inspiring voice. One last snort, another final shake of the head and one more final attempt to buck, and in an instant, I am settled in a blanket of warm understanding as I listen to His voice. With my ears pricked in fatal excitement and dangerous wonder, I finally hear what He is saying. From the words that were spoken to Job long ago in the time of the ancients, the Storm speaks unto me:

HAST, THOU GIVEN THE HORSE STRENGTH? HAST, THOU CLOTHED HIS NECK WITH THUNDER? CANST, THOU MAKE HIM AFRAID AS A GRASSHOPPER AND SPRING IN FEAR? THE GLORY OF HIS NOSTRILS IS TERRIBLE. HE PAWETH AT THE VALLEY AND REJOICETH IN HIS STRENGTH. HE GOETH ON TO MEET THE ARMED MEN. HE MOCKETH AT FEAR, AND IS NOT AFFRIGHTED; NEITHER TURNETH HE BACK FROM THE SWORD. THE QUIVER RATTLETH AGAINST HIM, THE GLITTERING SPEAR AND THE SHIELD. HE SWALLOWETH THE GROUND WITH FIERCENESS AND RAGE: NEITHER BELIEVETH HE THAT IT IS THE SOUND OF THE TRUMPET. HE SAITH AMONG THE TRUMPETS, HA, HA! AND HE SMELLETH THE BATTLE AFAR OFF! THE THUNDER OF THE CAPTAINS, AND THE SHOUTING.

Then the thunder roars again, and He speaks to me this very truth:

I AM YOUR FATHER AND YOU ARE MY CHILD. I CREATED YOU AND YOU BELONG TO ME. THIS PLATEAU HAS BEEN YOUR TEACHER, AND YOUR REBELLION HAS BEEN YOUR SONG. YOU HAVE RUN THE GROUND HERE UNBRIDLED AND WITHOUT CAUSE, AND ALL OF THIS BECAUSE I WOULD HAVE IT SO. FOR MY SAKE YOU ARE HERE. FOR MY PURPOSE YOU ARE ALONE ON THIS PLATEAU, FOR I CREATED THE WIND ON WHICH YOU RIDE AND THE FIRE IN YOUR BELLY THAT MAKES YOU CHARGE. I EVEN CREATED YOUR REBELLION FOR MY PURPOSE, AND NOW IS THE DAY I REVEAL IT TO YOU. YOU ARE MY SON; YOU ARE THE SON OF THUNDER, AND THE LIGHTNING IS NOW YOUR CAUSE. THE LIGHTNING IS MY POWER AND NOW YOU WILL BECOME FULLY AWARE OF ITS PURPOSE FOR YOU! FROM THIS DAY FORWARD, YOU HAVE BECOME MY WARHORSE AND YOU WILL NOW OBEY MY THUNDER AND YOU WILL NOW TAKE MY LIGHTNING AND SHOW IT TO THIS WICKED WORLD. FOR THERE IS LIFE FOR ALL IN THE LIGHTNING AND THE THUNDER CHOOSES WHO IT WILL GIVE! NOW YOU KNOW YOUR PURPOSE AND NOW YOU WILL TRULY LIVE! WITH MY BRIDLE IN YOUR MOUTH AND MY REINS AROUND YOUR NECK, YOU WILL WAR NO MORE FOR THE WORLD, NOW YOU WILL WAR FOR ME! WHEN I SAY GO, YOU WILL CHARGE. WHEN I SAY RIGHT, YOU WILL TURN. WHEN I SAY SNORT, YOU WILL SHOOT OUT YOUR MIGHTY BREATH AND YOU WILL BE HEARD. FOR I WILL SPEAK THROUGH YOU AND YOU WILL BE IN OBEDIENCE TO ME AND NOW YOU WILL LIVE! MIGHTY WARHORSE; THUNDER IN YOUR MANE, POWER IN MY NAME, GLORY IN YOUR STRIDE AND MERCY AT YOUR SIDE YOU WILL FOREVER BE ON A NEW PLATEAU I GIVE YOU TO RESIDE. THIS WILL BE YOUR NEW HOME; A PLACE WHERE YOU NOW CAN ROAM. THIS PLATEAU RESTS AT THE FOOT

OF MY HOLY MOUNTAIN, A PLACE YOU WILL NEVER AGAIN HAVE TO RUN ALONE. FOR NOW, MY SON, WHEN IT'S TIME TO RUN, LORD JESUS WILL MOUNT UP WITH A SHOUT AND SAY, "THUNDER HORSE…LET'S RIDE!"

SONS AND DAUGHTERS OF THUNDER

A farewell to all
And to all a good night
My old life is over
Buried by the light
No traces to be recovered
Death of the old man
Only new creation now
With fire in my hand
Mighty man of God
Out of the ashes of cold death
Old man cast away
As far as the east is from the west
Son of Thunder is rising
Like the sun each new day
Gaining power and knowledge
To carry God's sword to slay
Holy War on Addiction
Is now my battle cry
Bible thumping believer
Jesus freak do or die
For death is just my passage
Only true death can now say
Addiction make your arrangements
Destruction is headed your way
We already claim Victory
Now we just have to spread the word
Take our charge to every battlefield
Our battle cry must be heard
In search of our lost family
Brothers and sisters desperately in need
The trumpet has sounded

Jesus is coming to set you free
All you lonely drug addicts
Just hold on for another day
The Sons and Daughters of Thunder Army
Is headed your way
Don't worry we will find you
For we ourselves were you before
We know where you are pinned down
Where death is knocking at your door
Jesus is leading our Army
He will never leave one behind
Hold on and never give up
Fight on and hold the front line
We are coming with reinforcements
To relieve you from your post
Once we locate your position
You will be saved by the Holy Ghost
His power will grab you quickly
As your brothers and sisters arrive
We will all gather together
We will bring you out alive
Sons and Daughters of Thunder
We have come to collect our own
You are our family
In Christ Jesus we will bring you home
For He has already triumphed in Victory
No longer on the battlefield you will lay
We will bring you into His sanctuary
Come to Thunder House and stay
For you have fought the good fight
You have earned the right to find
A place you can call your home
Come and rest, relax your mind
Come and heal your broken body

Let Jesus love your spirit back to life
No more lonely addiction
Cutting through your soul like an angry knife
Let God pick up the broken pieces
It is time for you to find some much needed rest
Only in Christ Jesus is this possible
Come to Thunder House and your soul will be eternally blessed

FACE TO FACE

Two prisoners sitting across from each other
One silently pondering things unseen
I am the one lost in my own thoughts
Cold steel table hardness it always brings
In a dorm full of chaos
Iron doors cement walls echoes of fear
A question is asked by one
How do you know when God's spirit is here
In that sacred moment
The promising question asked I ran through my mind
Surely I can come up with a good answer
Somewhere rattling around in my head a smart word I can find
Searching for this savory morsel of knowledge
Some sweet nugget tasty and fresh
My mind takes me inside a picture
The place where humanity was eternally blessed
Standing in awe of my surroundings
Lost in my mind found at the foot of the cross
Unable to put into words
The price my sweet Jesus it cost
His innocent blood spilled with great abuse
Pain upon pain relentlessly repeated
Misery delivered by the hands of wickedness
The place where sin was triumphantly defeated
Our heavy burden that day was lifted
His pierced body sadly lowered from the cross
The day the world eclipsed darkness
On Calvary evil and wickedness has lost
Unknowingly they have killed their king
They have slain Almighty God's only begotten Son
The one and only savior

In Him is eternal life for all who will ever come
For me I was pulled from a darkness
The hand of Jesus reaching into a stinking pit
Pulled from the burning fire of my addiction
In freedom at a steel table now I sit
He delivered me into this prison
Here He knew I would finally listen to His voice
He led me to its chapel
In Him there I learned to rejoice
He taught me the meaning of praise and worship
Through His Spirit a better way I have been shown
He brought me into His righteousness
Covered me with it like a beautiful new flowing robe
He gave me a new found confidence
Stripped away all my old filthy clothes
His love walked me into freedom
He gave me new seed to sow
Life-giving water to nourish
A new song streaming sweet melody from my mouth
His word hot seared burned into my heart
How great is our God I began to scream and shout
More exciting than scoring the game-winning touchdown
Much better than winning the lottery one lucky day
Having discovered Christ's unending love
Nothing of this world can compare to His way
For His way is so lovely
His burden is ever so light
His yoke I have taken upon me
Put an end to this life's meaningless fight
Sitting here in this prison
True freedom in Jesus I have found
His love for me endured at the cross
Throughout my soul His sacrifice abounds
Sitting here at this cold hard steel table

Face to Face the question asked by my friend
How do you know when God's spirit is here
I began to tell him it's like the wind
Then in my ear a silent whisper
His still soft voice resting over me
Jesus said invite me to come sit at the table
I will open your hearts so you can clearly see
I stopped with my fancy description
Immediately in prayer I asked Jesus to come in
Like mighty rushing waters invading
A wave of Holy Love by the whirlwind He did send
Glistening down rain pour of His Holy Spirit
Showering down upon us we were totally consumed
Taking all words and our breath from us
It seemed like just the two of us were left in the once crowded room
Grace abounding in the moment
Our spirits lifted on wings of light from above
White Flag full surrender our hearts
Surrounded now by His blazing unconditional love
Resonating Holiness through my inner being
My spirit dancing in rhythm with my glorious King
God gave us the gift of His Holy presence
The true reality my best explanation could never bring
Cold hard steel table set on fire
Forever capturing my once bleeding heart
This the moment I fell in love with Jesus
In prison at a table the day His Holy Love gave spark
He ignited our bosoms with consuming fire
Burning hot love bright light into our souls
Now as we are able to speak
Off our tongues no words able to roll
Sitting in golden silence
Only our eyes able to speak the truth

God sent His Holy Spirit to answer
Over our table His blinding love He let loose
Love me tender forever
Love us sweet saving Holy Grace
The day I fell in love with Jesus
In a prison at a cold hard steel table I came Face to Face!

NO EGG NOG THIS YEAR

I have fallen again
Locked up in a hole
Christmas is here
Jingle bells once again the enemy stole
I am a prisoner
Held captive in my own mind
Razor wire fences
No Christmas cheer to find
Put out from the world
Feel like a forgotten castaway
Christmas is here again
Can I make it through this day?
My family is celebrating
Singing Christmas carols to hear
All I can listen to
Metal to metal echoing fear
How do I do Christmas?
As a prisoner to sin
Santa Claus and his reindeer
Don't have proper clearance to get in
Now I must suffer
Sitting dejected on my bunk
Memories of Christmas past
No eggnog to be drunk
No Christmas tree to trim
No stockings to be filled
Just me and my new family
Held here against our will
Stuck in this mind frame
Negativity at its best
Now I must focus
On Christmas' true greatest gift

It's all about Jesus
The rest just distraction in the wind
Trying to take my focus away
Keeping me locked up in pretend
Santa Claus is coming
It's all about who gets the best gift
Christmas parties on high
Let's get lost in holiday bliss
This year can be different
The year it finally sinks in
Unable to celebrate with the world
A grateful prisoner locked within
Now I can focus
On the only thing I have left
Jesus Christ my Lord and Savior
This year I received the greatest gift

LOST AT SEA

Alone at sea as a wanderer
Adrift now lost track of time
Sun scorched and without guidance
A prisoner of this ocean and my mind
Lost on the waters of self-reliance
With a paddle made out of broken dreams
Frantically calling for anyone
Please come hurry and rescue me
How lonely is this ocean?
Once your arms are all paddled out
Sitting perched on pieces of wreckage
Sharks circling to feed on my doubts
The ship that sailed me into my bright future
Now has dreadfully fallen apart
Smashed by the storm of my addiction
Not at all what I had intended from the start
Searching the painful horizon
No signs of life can be found
Waves are crashing in tragic melody
Chords of regret making ominous sounds
God's mighty spirit is calling
The giver of light to all things
Holy Spirit always shining forth
Beacon to all lost human beings
A lighthouse standing tall on a cliff
For all His lost ships at sea
The mark of His safe harbor
A place of rest and peace for you and me
A compass of sure direction
He is the wind that makes me come about
He delivers power into my sails

He is a rudder of guidance in the midst of my doubt
God has given me a new vessel
This ship will for sure sail me home
Headed back navigated by His glory
No longer do I travel alone
Now as I turn for safety
Only His spirit knows the way
I am headed for God's safe harbor
Now the waves finally obey
The stars have become my music
Dancing across the beautiful night
The bear jumps over Orion
My new heading takes off in flight
No more wasted movements
No need for orange life vests
God has now taken over my journey
Giving this sailor much needed rest
My life is now good weather
In this ocean I am no longer alone
Sailing along in calm waters
Pointed towards Jesus who will carry me home

THROUGH THE FIRE

God is a sword
Sharp cutting through your life
Light overcoming darkness
Measured in your eyes
His voice speaks softly to you
Booming thunder heard throughout
Beat on a drum in rhythm
Worship, praise, sing, dance and shout
For all glory is for God
In Christ Jesus the only way through
A wall of fire flaming swords
Stands between Heaven and you
This world has fallen
Corrupted and polluted by sin
This world is a furnace
You must be purified by affliction from within
A vessel made for His spirit
Pure and Holy you must become
Only by walking through the furnace with Jesus
Will ever get the job done
For this life in the physical
Living each day in the flesh is in vain
True riches are found in the spiritual
The difference between Abel and Cain
For Abel's sacrifice was worthy
Cain's God did detest
The world keeps on killing
A worthy sacrifice to God is our self
Give your life over to Jesus
The only way this can be done
The only way back to the Father in Spirit
Is by walking through the fire with the only begotten Son

VI. SHINE

ROMANS 16:20 (NKJV)
And the god of peace will crush satan under your feet shortly.

MATTHEW 4:8-11 (NKJV)
Again, the devil took him up on an exceedingly high mountain, and showed him all the kingdoms of the world and their glory. And he said to him, "all these things I will give you if you will fall down and worship me." Then Jesus said to him, "away with you, satan! For it is written, 'you shall worship the LORD your god, and him only you shall serve.'" then the devil left him, and behold, angels came and ministered to him.

MATTHEW 5:14-16 (NKJV)
"You are the light of the world. A city that is set on a hill cannot be hidden. Nor do they light a lamp and put it under a basket, but on a lampstand, and it gives light to all who are in the house. Let your light so shine before men, that they may see your good works and glorify your father in heaven.

Satan, or the devil, uses the weapon of addiction—the weakness in our flesh and carnal minds—along with the magical properties of alcohol and drugs to try to gain access to our souls. God instructs us to stay sober and vigilant because we are under attack. The devil prowls around the earth like a roaring lion looking for someone to devour. He does this through alcohol and drugs. The devil wants our souls. The devil's trap of addiction, fueled by alcohol and drugs, seeks to undermine God's plan of redemption for humanity. It clouds our understanding of who we are as His precious children and blinds us with a lie about the Truth—that the Word came to us in the flesh as the only begotten Son, Jesus Christ, to redeem us. By believing in Jesus, we can find our way back to our Heavenly Father and live with Him in His Kingdom of Heaven forever.

JOHN 14:6 (NKJV)

Jesus said to him, "I am the way, the truth, and the life. No one comes to the Father except through Me.

Three times in my life, and all when I was at the lowest points possible in my addiction, Satan himself appeared to me in the spiritual realm. He manipulated me in my addiction to create a perfect environment using a portal of spiritual wickedness to open me up to the spiritual realm, where he could show himself to me and make me an offer. The fasting for days and sometimes weeks, lack of sleep, and "witches brew" of manufactured chemicals in the drugs all worked together as he planned. He showed himself and spoke to me through another person he had entered. Each time he did this, my spiritual eyes were opened to a vision of his wickedness, where he was able to perpetrate his ultimate proposition, which was that he alone was the only one that could deliver me out of this horrible pit I was in and make me prosper in this unforgiving drug culture I had found myself trapped within.

LUKE 22:3 (NKJV)

Then satan entered Judas, surnamed Iscariot, who was numbered among the twelve.

The first time he revealed himself to me was in 1999 in Denver, Colorado. I was in a crack house in the projects with the "Egg-Man," as he was cutting crack rocks. When he slid the rocks over to me, they looked like demon heads to me, and they seemed alive and animated, laughing and mocking me, as if they knew I was under their control. Satan, through the "Egg-Man," said nothing but looked at me and smiled, only showing his wickedness and seemingly trying to instill fear in me. As I shared in an earlier chapter, he succeeded in the fear part and scared me so badly that I nearly murdered the people in the room by stabbing them in the necks with a steak knife I had hidden in my front pocket. Fortunately, the enemy failed in this attempt to destroy me. Thank you, Jesus!

The second time he appeared to me, I was sitting at a table in an apartment in Tucson, Arizona. The place was run down and in total disarray, and the man and woman who lived there were about to be evicted and were destitute, looking for more drugs. This time, I was sitting at a table with the couple who lived there and another man whose nickname was "Slim". Slim was the man who was with me when I was arrested for shoplifting at the grocery store, and the police officer let me go, and I walked down the street and stole the Red Mustang. I was sitting at the table in their "cracked-out" apartment, and the room began to change, and I began to see Satan coming through all three people at the table. As each one would talk, Satan would come through them, and I could see him in their faces and hear his voice in my mind as they would speak. They were sitting there, and my spiritual eyes had opened, and I could see them, but could also see the devil in them and hear the devil speaking to me as if he were right there in the room. He began moving from person to person, saying different things to me through each of them. He would move to one person and say something, then jump to another and say something, and then move on to another, and I kept following him and listening to him speak, letting his words sink in to my mind. It was such a twisted moment; it seemed to me that I was hearing him talk audibly in my ears, even though it was just in my mind. These are the schemes and wiles of the devil spoken about in Ephesians 6:11. It also talks about the armor of God in the same chapter, and that night, I had zero armor and no helmet of salvation. I was helpless prey, and I made myself that way by smoking drugs.

As they started talking, I could physically hear their voices, but I also heard the enemy's voice and understood his words in my mind. During this exchange, he began speaking to my mind arrogantly, trying to convince me that he was something special and that I was nothing—just a weak, scum-of-the-earth crackhead, and the people with me were the lowest of the low in society. He told me I was just like them and described how far my life had fallen and how low I had become. He claimed he had all this power and could do incredible things. I remember feeling an overwhelming sense of arrogance and pride emanating from him—something I had never felt before. As he insulted me and exposed how broken my life was, he also spoke negatively about everything around me, positioning himself above everything. He pointed out how dirty the house I was in was and how unkempt and nasty all of us sitting around the table looked. It made me feel awful and small. This is his only tactic: the devil will gain access to your soul through the drugs, then speak to your mind, pushing you and everything around down, so he can rise above it all. This is his game plan. He never changes; he is always the same. His only desire is to exalt himself above God, His throne, and us who are created in the image of God. His ultimate aim is for us to bow down and worship him, just as he tempted Jesus to do in the desert. The next part of his plan is for us to give him our souls so he can become an indwelling spirit, further trying to imitate God. Satan, or the devil, wants to be God, and he wants children of his own. Just as men and women who believe in Jesus invite Jesus into their hearts, Satan also wants to trick men and women into inviting him into theirs.

This second appearance was different from the first, where he had tried to instill fear in me. During this encounter, the devil began to speak to me and introduced himself as something special, trying to impress me with his exploits and cleverness. The thing I remember most about this encounter was his arrogance, smugness, boasting, and contempt. I did the only thing I knew to do at the time, and I started crying out to God in my mind, pleading for Him to come and save me. I kept repeating in my mind, "I belong to Jesus, I belong to Jesus, I belong to Jesus!"

My third and final encounter with Satan took place in a crack house in Austin, Texas, where I had been frequenting as I moved from one drug house to another in search of crack—the poison and medicine I needed to escape my reality. That night, I found myself trapped in the darkest moment of my life, and this time, the devil appeared to me as an angel of light. The relentless onslaught of alcohol and drugs, combined with overwhelming emotional stress, pain, misery, hopelessness, feelings of complete defeat, and exhaustion from sleep deprivation, fasting, and ongoing spiritual attack, created the perfect environment for his ultimate proposition. I was broken and held captive by my addiction in the depths of darkness—the blackest darkness I had ever known. My weakened spirit, tormented soul, and shattered mind worked together to set me up, the addict, for this carefully planned and long-awaited encounter at the crossroads of my spiritual life. Satan had been working on this for 25 years, pushing me toward the point where he could make his final, golden offer. He was patient in his craft, strategic in his purpose, and relentless in his pursuit. That is the entire purpose of addiction—this is the endgame. From the very beginning, when Satan implanted his weapon of addiction within me, this was always the destination he planned for me to reach. This was Satan's perfect storm!

JOHN 10:27-29 (NKJV)

My sheep hear my voice, and I know them, and they follow me. And I give them eternal life, and they shall never perish; neither shall anyone snatch them out of my hand. My father, who has given them to me, is greater than all, and no one is able to snatch them out of my father's hand. I and my father are one."

The devil uses our addiction to drugs to eventually lead us into a spiritually wicked vision, where he can reveal himself and make his offer. You must stop playing with this hellish fire now—it's an evil game you'll never win, and a war is being fought for your soul that will determine your eternal destiny. I don't know how else to say it. These alcohol and drugs are not our friends; they are enemies and weapons designed to steal our souls from Almighty God. The enemy can only take your soul by tricking you into giving it to him or by dying in your sins without Jesus Christ and the Holy Spirit. He will use addiction to weaken you over time, making you vulnerable to his deception. He will lead you into the deepest, darkest pit and appear as a savior. Remember, Satan wants to be God. He wants our souls for himself. He desires his children and an eternal kingdom to rule. He knows his future—where he will be chained in hell for eternity—and he seeks to drag as many of us with him as he can.

If you continue in your addiction, be advised that this encounter will eventually happen to you if you do not find death first. This meeting with the devil is your final destination and the enemy of your soul's desired outcome. He put this plan into play in your life a long time ago, when he first seeded addiction within you and disguised it as fun and excitement when you first started experimenting with drugs and alcohol. This is the TRUTH! You must come to terms with the knowledge and understanding that this has happened and continues to happen in your life. You must understand that there is only one true Savior for your soul, and that one is Jesus Christ. You must realize the truth that the only way to overcome your addiction is by surrendering your life to Jesus Christ and becoming His disciple. The only way out of the darkness is by the Light of Jesus Christ. You must gain godly wisdom and know that only Jesus, through the Holy Spirit, can provide you with your spiritual armor to protect yourself against future attacks. When you become His disciple, He will equip you with spiritual armor and weaponry that will help you defeat the enemy and destroy the weapon of addiction, once and for all. He will show you how to defeat the prince of the power of the air.

The enemy will never quit or stop trying to trick you into giving up your soul to him, destroying you. The enemy never sleeps and is a master deceiver. We are no match for him alone. If the enemy has succeeded in catching you with addiction once, he will return to do so again and again. He disguises it each time, trying to get you to take one more bite of the tasty apple of your sinful desire. That juicy lie that tastes so good to your flesh. The enemy will never rest and will keep presenting addiction to you on a silver platter, hoping you'll partake again. Maybe this time, he will be the one time he can finally claim victory by invading your soul through an invitation from you, when he appears as a savior disguised as an angel of light.

"The Devil can counterfeit all the saving operations and graces of the Spirit of God." ~ Jonathan Edwards

This will lead to your destruction, and you will inevitably spend eternity with him as his child in hell. If you take away only one message from this book, let it be that this is a serious business of the most serious kind. The drugs and alcohol you are using can be turned against you to determine the eternal fate of your soul. Playing with substances we become addicted to has a darker, more sinister side than what appears on the surface. Many have fallen and lost their souls to the enemy by being tricked and deceived in this way. Do not be another victim! Do not be the next fool! Do not be the next fish caught on the devil's line with a big hook in your mouth. Make a decision to stop this madness today! Heed my warning and listen to this TRUTH! Only Jesus Christ can set us free from the captivity, darkness, and hell caused by addiction, and only His eternal Light can bring the Truth, Power, Love, Hope, and Forgiveness that deliver, heal, and cure us from our chained and addicted lives. Step out of darkness now, into His marvelous Light!

1 PETER 2:9 (NKJV)
But you are a chosen generation, a royal priesthood, a holy nation, His own special people, that you may proclaim the praises of Him who called you out of darkness into His marvelous light

In my weakened and demoralized state in a crack house in Austin, Texas, Satan came to me once again for the third time. To prepare me for his arrival, he had me go back to the crack house where I had the experience where I thought I had died and gone to hell that I wrote about in the first chapter, "How Did I Die?". This time, when I arrived at the crack house, the same man and woman who were in the room when I thought I had died were in the room again. They were sitting in the same room as before and smoking crack, and I had brought some as well. The man was a guy who seemed to have success in the crack game with a beautiful woman, plenty of money, and always had drugs. Interestingly, the first time I saw this woman walk into the room and sit down across from me, I was immediately attracted to her. I believe the enemy was using her then, as bait to create an opportunity to influence me for this future encounter.

That night, the man showed me how he could have total control over this woman by administering the crack to her. I was standing in the kitchen, and he said to me, "Come over here and watch this." He told me to light the flame as he held the pipe to the woman's lips, and as she inhaled the smoke, she went into a trance of sorts, and I was captured in the moment. It aroused my curiosity as to what this could be and how this was so different from any reaction or experience I had ever seen of someone smoking crack. I had never before in all my years of smoking crack ever seen this before or ever seen someone go into a trance like this from smoking crack. This trance was sensual and very seductive, and it appeared to me that this man had total control over this woman. I believe that the enemy was setting another hook into me, showing me this in preparation for his final offer. I believe that the devil thought that in my desperation, I would desire to have this same kind of power over women and finally be able to use the crack instead of the crack using me. In his craftiness, I believe the devil thought that he could get me into a deep, dark hole of confusion and despair that would give him the perfect time and opportunity to make me an attractive proposition. The devil would give me perceived dominion and control over the crack cocaine that, up until now, had ruled over me like a tyrant, in exchange for my soul. He thought that I would desire this power for myself and be desperate enough to accept his deal.

After the woman finished smoking crack, the man led her into the other room, and we sat down on the couch. He then stood in front of us and started to speak. At that moment, my spiritual eyes opened, and I saw a vision of Satan coming through the man, just as he had done before when I was at a table full of people in Tucson. As the man spoke, I could see Satan in the man's face, and I could hear Satan's voice in my mind through the man's spoken words. Here it is! Now was the time that the enemy had chosen to make a play for my soul. He told me that he would share everything with me, including the woman, and that he would show me how to use crack and be successful with it—selling it and using it without becoming a desperate, weakened crack addict. He claimed I could use crack to gain power instead of letting it ruin me, if I allowed him to do in me what he was doing in the man standing before me. Then he made me an offer he thought I couldn't refuse. I believe the devil had been preparing me for this moment for many years, grooming me for his ultimate proposition, and this was the perfect time for him to strike when I was at my lowest and darkest place I had ever been in my life.

1 PETER 5:8 (NKJV)

Be sober, be vigilant; because your adversary the devil walks about like a roaring lion, seeking whom he may devour.

The offer he made to me was this: if I would let him use my body and soul so that he could come in and shine, then when he came through me and shined, I would shine also. He said if I would give him my soul and let him enter my body, he would give me the cunning and craftiness to rise out of the darkness where I was now stranded. He said his shine could elevate me within this wicked drug culture, just like he was showing me how he was doing for the man standing in front of me, the one who had put the woman in the trance. Satan, the snake of all snakes, told me he would shine through me, and because of him, the people in this dark drug world would see him and be attracted to him, and also to me. He said he would take me to the top of the game, and I would rise out of the pit I was in, and get people to do whatever I wanted, and I would always have crack and methamphetamine and would never again have any problem acquiring drugs. He would take care of all the details, and I would finally be free to do whatever I wanted with drugs. He said these words to me as he did a vaudeville side shuffle dance, "You see, when I shine…You shine!"

The man that the devil was speaking through, I believe, was faced with this same proposition at one point in his life and accepted it. This person, to me, in my desperation, seemed to have it all together and appeared as if he had mastered the drug called crack cocaine, something that had ruled over me and caused me so much pain and misery for so many years. Just as Satan came to Eve through the serpent, Satan came to me through one of his servants to offer me a lie he thought I was ready to believe in my utter weakness and pitch-black, darkened state. When Satan came through the man, I knew exactly who he was without him having to say, because I had encountered him twice before. What Satan failed to realize is that I belong to Jesus Christ, and when I am weak, I am strong because, in my weakness, Jesus' power rests on and over me. I believe that Jesus has always been with me since before He knitted me in my mother's womb, and He protected me all these years in my addiction because He knew one day I would surrender my life to Him. Jesus says not one that belongs to Him will be plucked from His hand, and I have always been one of His, and if you are reading this, so are you! You see, I have always been God's evangelist and His witness to the end of the earth. I was just out of position, but always under the protection of His wings.

PSALM 91:3-4 (NIV)

Surely, he will save you from the fowler's snare and from the deadly pestilence. He will cover you with his feathers, and under his wings you will find refuge; his faithfulness will be your shield and rampart.

There is no light in Satan, only darkness. Satan is all smoke and mirrors and will even use your own light to reflect off of him back to you, making you think he has light. Satan, the enemy of God, intruder, imitator, deceiver, thief, destroyer, and wicked one, can only flash or mimic light, as he did when he appeared to me in visions. A flash is not real; it is merely a reflection, a deception, and a theft from another light source, or a trick to deceive us in our darkened state, causing us to believe we are seeing real light when there is none. Satan is an illusionist, masquerading as an angel of light with his deceptions, lies, sorceries, and dark magic. He is an impersonator and a cheap knockoff of the only true Light source, which is Jesus Christ. Satan uses alcohol and drugs to blind us and push us deeper into darkness, so when he appears, he resembles a light. The deeper into darkness he can drive you, the easier it is for him to deceive you. The devil is a liar!

2 CORINTHIANS 11:14 (NIV)
And no wonder, for Satan himself masquerades as an angel of light.

2 CORINTHIANS 4:4-7 (NLT)
Satan, who is the god of this world, has blinded the minds of those who don't believe. They are unable to see the glorious light of the good news. They don't understand this message about the glory of Christ, who is the exact likeness of God. You see, we don't go around preaching about ourselves. We preach that Jesus Christ is lord, and we ourselves are your servants for Jesus' sake. For God, who said, "let there be light in the darkness," has made this light shine in our hearts so we could know the glory of God that is seen in the face of Jesus Christ. We now have this light shining in our hearts, but we ourselves are like fragile clay jars containing this great treasure. This makes it clear that our great power is from God, not from ourselves.

There is only one True Light in the spiritual realm, and that Light is the Love of Jesus Christ, which is all-powerful. Jesus Christ is the Light that entered this dark world to give Light to all who believe in Him and accept Him as Lord and Savior. His Light pierces through the darkness of drug addiction and sin. There is no light in the devil—only darkness, lies, and deception. He is an imitator who disguises himself as an angel of light. He displays false light as bait to tempt us. The devil used this same tactic when he tempted Jesus in the wilderness, and Jesus, the Light who entered the world, responded with the Word of God and the Truth to rebuke him and forced the devil to flee. We must do the same!

Always remember the schemes and tricks of that flashy devil and his pack of lies. Flash is fake—a cheap counterfeit made to look like the real thing, but never actually does when you take a closer look. Flash is designed to catch your attention and is used to temporarily blind you. Flash is not authentic and should never be mistaken for Shine! Shine is eternal, and only Jesus Christ can Shine; when He Shines, it is through those who belong to Him and have made Him their Lord and Savior, surrendering their lives to the one True Light.

This is the end of the road in the drug game, when the spiritual realm opens before you, and Satan himself appears subtly before your spiritual eyes, having come for your soul. Satan makes his final move when you have lost all hope and find yourself in utter darkness, with your body broken down by drugs, and no sleep or food. I believe that some of you reading this right now have gone as deep as I have into the dark, lonely pit of addiction and have had similar experiences. For those of you who have, please speak out and share your story with others, warning them. For those who haven't, please be aware of this spiritual component linked to addiction and drug use. Continuing down this path will either result in dying in your unrepentant sins and being lost in hell or having an encounter with the devil, who will ask for your soul. This is a guarantee.

Thanks be to God that my Lord and Savior Jesus Christ kept me from accepting the evil invitation offered to me by Satan. At that moment, when I was about to answer yes or no, Jesus shut my mouth completely. I could not say a word either way, even if I wanted to. That's my God. That's my Jesus. That's my protector, my fortress, my stronghold, and my deliverer, my shield, in whom I take refuge. Thank you, Lord, for having other plans for my soul rather than wasting my life living in the darkness of addiction, serving sin, and giving away what is precious to You and trading it in for a cheap imitation. Thank you for not allowing me to be plucked from your hand and believing a bold-faced lie from the father of all lies. In the name of Jesus Christ, I rebuke you, Satan. Get thee hence, get behind me, get under my feet now, and depart from me and from all those who are reading this book now or those who will read it in the future. We all belong to the King of Kings, the One True Light that shines and makes the darkness flee, the all-powerful Jesus Christ, who is over all things, including you. Only Jesus Christ can make us shine, and I am happy to say today, **"When Jesus shines...He shines through me!"**

SHINE!!!

Lightning in a bottle
Bright shining star
Heavenly splendor
Can I put it in a jar
My God
Look what you have done
The lights shining in the firmament
How you hung the sun
Diamonds sparkle
Facets of shining bright
A lesson from the moon
Reflection of sun's blazing light
Powerful, Magnificent, Glorious
Constellations moving through space
Sun-fed rainbow prism
Beautiful shining angel's face
Nuclear fusion
Blows my mind
Exploding fire
Cold stare to make the eye blind
Synapses communicate
Electricity in the brain
Charges shining
How can you explain
Information travels
On the wings of brilliant light
The brighter the better
Measured pinpoint tight
One little match
Can chase away the dark
A mighty standing forest

Destroyed by just one spark
The stars at night
Are big and bright
Lonesome campfire cowboy
Sings deep in the heart they shine
Is it possible to say
I can shine like the day
Can I shine from within
Is Jesus the light to all men
I open up my heart
My faith given to the blind
Now looking for Jesus
What will I find...
He found me
His spirit quickly rushing in
On the wings of pure light
By the way of the whirlwind
My body does a little shake
As the electricity begins to hum
Full of massive amounts of energy
Like I just swallowed the bright orange sun
Jesus' light has certainly blessed
God's grace can surely attest
It's the spirit of truth
Falling on me like the sunset in the west
His shine indeed can be captured
For I am that jar
His brilliance displayed
Jesus Christ the bright morning star
His truth has been received
His grace on wings has set me free
Now as Jesus shines...
He shines through me!!!

VII. MY HOLY WAR ON ADDICTION

EXODUS 15:2-3 (NKJV)

The Lord is my strength and song, and He has become my salvation; He is my God, and I will praise Him; My father's God, and I will exalt Him. **THE LORD IS A MAN OF WAR;** the Lord is His name.

PSALM 144:1-2 (NKJV)

Blessed be the Lord my Rock, **WHO TRAINS MY HANDS FOR WAR, AND MY FINGERS FOR BATTLE**. My lovingkindness and my fortress, my high tower and my deliverer, my shield and the One in whom I take refuge, who subdues my people under me.

2 TIMOTHY 2:1-3 (NKJV)

You therefore, my son, be strong in the grace that is in Christ Jesus. And the things that you have heard from me among many witnesses, commit these to faithful men who will be able to teach others also. You therefore must endure hardship as **A GOOD SOLDIER OF JESUS CHRIST**.

Thank you, Jesus! Thank you, my God, for never leaving me or forsaking me and always being with me in my troubles. I traveled a very long road and grew weary in my journey through the captivity, darkness, and hell of addiction. I almost died so many times, but you were always there to keep my soul from going to hell. You reached down into my horrible addicted pit and brought me out into You. Even when I was at the lowest points in my life, sitting in crack houses in my utter despair and darkness, you were with me. You were with me because you wrote the beginning of the story of my life from the end, and you knew when you knit me in my mother's womb that I was your Disciple and Evangelist, I was your son!

PSALM 40:1-3 (NKJV)

I waited patiently for the LORD; and He inclined to me, and heard my cry. He also brought me up out of a horrible pit, out of the miry clay, and set my feet upon a rock, and established my steps. He has put a new song in my mouth - Praise to our God; many will see it and fear, and will trust in the LORD.

My journey through the captivity, darkness, and hell of addiction was a journey through death itself. The old addicted man that I had allowed myself to become had to die so the new man I am today could be reborn in his place as a disciple of Jesus Christ. God captured me at my lowest point in life, snatched me off the street, and sent me to prison. Behind bars, I finally surrendered all to Jesus Christ, and now I have been changed. Jesus brought me out of a drug-infested, horrible pit into Travis State Prison in the Texas Department of Criminal Justice for a one-year flat sentence. While incarcerated, I was finally able to surrender my life to Him, and I am changed. Jesus rescued me, delivered me, healed me, and showed me the truth that there is no addiction in Him and that His rest is the cure! In prison, I was able to repent of my sins, fully surrender to my God, and finally let the old addicted man inside me die.

When I surrendered my life to Him, God gave me the precious gift of His Holy Spirit. I became a new creation in Jesus Christ, which brought me to understand the truth, knowledge, and wisdom of who I am in Jesus as His victorious child. Jesus showed me that through Him and His Power, I have victory, complete authority, and dominion over all addictions, demonic spirits, principalities, and over my own flesh that was totally out of control and where my addiction set its hooks into me at an early age, sowing in me the wickedness of the darkness of this evil fallen world. I was blind, and now I see.

When I was filled with the Holy Spirit, the fire of God burned away my addiction and replaced my desire for drugs and alcohol with a new hunger for His presence. I put all my hope in Jesus, and He had to be who I was hoping He would be, or I was done. He was my only hope after trying everything in this world, and nothing ever worked except the same old failures, leading back to addiction and then prison. I am here to tell everyone that Jesus is far more than I could have ever imagined and has over-delivered on all I believed I was promised. I can't find the words to describe the life He has given me and how incredible it is!

I was released from prison on May 27, 2014, into a Christian Drug Rehabilitation Discipleship Home in Austin, Texas. Afterwards, I joined a Spirit-filled church where I was baptized, and the Lord began to teach me His ways. At the church, Pastor Tom Ravizza led a Celebrate Recovery Group, and I attended regularly, sharing my testimony on several occasions. That program helped ground me in the Lord during the year after my release from prison. My focus was on being obedient to God's Word and learning what it meant to follow Jesus. The Lord brought several amazing Men of God into my life during this period, who mentored and discipled me. Thank you, Bobby Barker, Jose Hernandez, Tom Cook, Mike Spradlin, and Tom Ravizza, for everything you have done for me. Where I am today in my walk with the Lord is a result of your ministering to me and the words of encouragement you poured into my life.

I want to share this incredible story about something only God can do. This will blow your mind! I am six weeks out of prison, and my mentor, Bobby Barker, invites me to a Prison Fellowship Conference in Columbus, Texas. He said he would pick me up at 5:30 am on Saturday and drive to Columbus. He also mentioned that he had arranged for me to share my testimony with the prison ministers who would be there. The weekend before this event, I visited my children at the house I had lived in before going to prison. At that time, their mother allowed me to see them on the weekends.

When I was there, I entered my old office and saw a rock on one of the shelves that held a lot of significance for me. Why was this rock so important? Let me explain. When I was first in prison in Arizona in 2008, I was at the Florence Unit. At this prison, we stayed in Army tents in the desert, surrounded by tall fences and razor wire. This area was just outside the walls of the central maximum-security prison. Next to the tents was a recreation yard with a track and basketball courts. When I felt stressed from being in prison, I would sometimes go out to the track and walk laps. The track was a mix of dirt and rocks, but it was suitable for walking and jogging, giving a decent workout.

One night, I was sitting in my housing area, which consisted of a bed and a small desk inside a tent that housed about 20 men, when the weight of my problems started pressing down on me. I could no longer handle the stress, so I went to the track to try to walk it off. It was already dark, but a few lights were still on, so I could walk and do laps. I started walking, trying to shake off the shame and guilt that covered me like a cold, wet blanket. It was a suffocating, depressing feeling. I began walking faster, trying to free myself from the darkness, but the faster I walked, the more suffocating I felt. Then, when I couldn't take it anymore, I yelled out loud, "Jesus, where are you?" As soon as I shouted at the top of my lungs, I stepped on something that caught my attention. It was a rock under my foot, so I bent down and picked it up. I was in a dark spot on the track and couldn't see it well. I moved over to a nearby light pole to get a better look. Once I was under the light and could see the rock clearly, I heard a voice say, "I AM RIGHT HERE WITH YOU, MICHAEL." That was when I noticed that the rock was shaped like Jesus' head, looking at him from the side and showing his profile. It was an exact profile of his head, with the outline of his mustache and beard, colored within the rock.

Beautiful shades of brown, gold, and red. It was incredible. I knew the voice was Jesus, and when I heard it, all the stress immediately melted away, and the shame and guilt disappeared, replaced by a warmth of love and hope in my heart. I just knew I would be okay—that Jesus was with me. He says in His word that He will never leave me nor forsake me, and in this moment, he reminded me of that promise.

This rock was a treasure to me, and I kept it with me at all times during my incarceration. It was approximately 2 inches wide and 4 inches tall, fitting nicely in the palm of my hand. It was my prized possession in a place where you are stripped of all your possessions upon entry. I held onto that rock with everything I had. It was my constant reminder that I was not alone in a very lonely, dark, and cruel prison. One day, a note arrived from the administration, instructing me to pack up my belongings, as I was being transferred to a new prison in Marana, Arizona. Immediately, I thought about my rock. There is no way they would let me take a rock out of this prison once I was processed for my move to Marana. A rock like that could be used as a weapon or to aid in an escape attempt by breaking locks or similar objects. I just knew I was going to lose my beautiful Jesus Rock. I decided to keep the rock with my belongings and said a prayer, asking Jesus to supernaturally hide the rock when they searched my belongings during the move. I went through processing, and they searched my things, bundled everything in a bag, and put the bag in a holding area on the transit bus. I was shackled and chained around my ankles and wrists and sent to a seat in the back. It was a long journey through the Arizona deserts from the Florence Unit to the Marana Unit. We made stops along the way and were put into a holding area at another prison, all the while I wondered if my rock had made the journey with me. Once I arrived at the Marana Unit and was processed, I was sent to my new housing unit. I opened my bag, and sure enough, my rock had made it. I was so excited. I knew Jesus had temporarily blinded them, both at the Florence Unit and now here at the Marana Unit, so they hadn't noticed my rock. That's the wonder-working power of Jesus Christ. I served my time in Marana, and when I was released, I said another prayer for my rock to come out with me, and it did. Thank you, Jesus. My dad met me outside the facility in a U-Haul, and I headed back to my home state of Texas with my Jesus Rock in hand.

Now, back in my old office at the house where I used to live before I went to prison, I saw the rock and immediately grabbed it from the shelf, holding it tightly in my hand. I remembered that Jesus will never leave me or forsake me—that He is always with me. I knew that rock was coming with me. So, when I left that day to go back to where I was staying, I took the rock with me. It felt like we were reunited again. When I returned to my sober-living discipleship home, I placed the rock on the table next to my bed to remind me of God's goodness. That week, leading up to the Prison Fellowship Conference, my Jesus Rock was there every night when I went to sleep and every morning when I woke. Once Saturday arrived, I heard a short honk of the horn, and it was Bobby there to pick me up. I headed for the door, but stopped in my tracks as a voice told me to grab the rock and take it with me. So, I went back to the table and picked up my Jesus Rock, putting it in my pocket. When I got in Bobby's truck, I told him about the rock in my pocket, and he thought it was cool, but he had no idea what was about to happen next. After I told Bobby about the rock and showed it to him, I put the rock back into my pocket and forgot about it.

From Austin, where we live, to Columbus, it's about a 1.5-hour drive. Bobby and I spent the trip talking about Jesus and how He has been so good to us. We were drinking coffee and enjoying an incredible drive. When we arrived at the church where the conference was being held, we went inside and started talking with everyone in attendance. I looked around and noticed a man who seemed familiar. I went over, said hello, and introduced myself. His name was Daniel

Ryczek. I told him he looked like someone who had ministered to me before and asked if he had ever served in ministry at the Travis County Jail or the Travis Unit Prison, where I had been incarcerated in Texas. He said he had never been to either place, so I thought I might have been mistaken. We kept talking, and he mentioned that he had moved from Arizona, and then it clicked. I realized he was my instructor at the Maricopa County Jail, where I earned a certificate of completion for the Acts program while I was there. Mr. Ryczek also became the Prison Chaplain at Florence Unit, where I found my Jesus Rock. I was shocked when I heard this and forgot that the Jesus Rock was in my pocket. We chatted for a bit longer, and then it was time for everyone to enter the sanctuary, to begin the conference. It was a wonderful day, with people sharing their prison ministry testimonies. Then it was my turn to speak, sharing how I surrendered my life to Jesus in prison and telling the prison ministers how much they had impacted my transformation.

    I took the stage, walked up behind the podium, and introduced myself. Then I remembered the rock in my pocket and the man I had just met—the Chaplain of the Prison where I found my Jesus rock—and I knew that God had brought us both there to share this story. Can you imagine the odds of something like this ever happening? How on earth did God get that rock from a prison yard in Arizona to a Prison Ministry Conference in Columbus, Texas, to be shared five years later? Only God can do this. After I introduced myself, I told the crowd that I had something in my pocket, and it was amazing that it was there. How could this rock be in my pocket under these circumstances? Unbelievable! So, I pulled the rock out, held it high, and shared the story of how I found it, what it meant to me, and the incredible journey it took to be where it was that day. Then I pointed to Brother Ryczek and told everyone about our connection—everyone was amazed at what God had done. I stepped down from the stage, handed the Jesus Rock to Daniel, hugged him, and told him that this rock was for him—reminding him of the lives he had helped change through his service to God.

What a beautiful story of how God moves in our lives and will never leave us or forsake us. But the story isn't over. Four years later, I received a gift. When I opened it up, I began to cry. It was a wooden box that clearly showed someone had taken great care and time to make. I opened the beautiful box, and nestled in scarlet velvet was my Jesus Rock. Above the box, when you lifted the lid, was a silver plaque that read, "Remember Where You Found Me." There was also a small note from Daniel Ryzcek that said, "I wanted to return your rock to you. Thank you for letting me hold it for a while." Boom! Full circle — my Jesus Rock came back to me, reminding me that He will never leave me or forsake me. Now, my Jesus Rock rests in its open box on a table in my house, so everyone who enters my home can see it, and I can share in this incredible story of love and hope. If God can give me Jesus Rock, He can do anything. What do you believe He can do for you if you give your life to Him as I have?

I have now been out of prison for about two months. I am still living in a discipleship home. I have joined a spirit-filled church, and Bobby comes to my house early every morning to pick me up and take me to the morning prayer group at the church. A group of us prays for about an hour for ourselves, our families, and our church. In our group, I have become friends with several people. One man in particular, Jose Hernandez, sometimes pulls me aside and ministers to me. At that time, I didn't have a steady job. After the prayer group in the morning, Bobby would take me to get something to eat, then drop me off at day labor, where I go out on various jobs and do the work, collecting a check at the end of the day. You would sit in the lobby area and wait for them to call out your name and your job for the day. One morning, I was in the lobby, and the lady asked everyone if they wanted a job holding a sign on the side of the road for a store having a sale. We call it "flying a sign." To my surprise, no one raised their hand, and I was right there with them. It was summer in Texas, over 100 degrees outside, and the last place you'd want to be was outside on the side of the road. No thanks. Then I felt the Holy Spirit nudge me to raise my hand. Believe me, I didn't want to do that work, but I raised my hand anyway. So off to the job I went.

It was an arduous journey to get there. I had to take three different buses to reach the shopping mall, then go inside and find the store with the sale. When I arrived, they handed me a sign and told me to go out onto the street and start waving it around. Keep in mind, I have a college degree and the background to do many other things besides flying a sign on the side of the road. But at that moment, I was happy and relieved that I wasn't still in prison. Plus, I had headphones on and was listening to Christian music, so I was already doing praise and worship anyway.

So, I went out to the street, and I had a great time flying my sign. I guess I was having so much fun that the people on the street corner, begging for money, told me to go away because I was messing up their business. I told them, God bless, and moved down to the other light to fly my sign. Just then, I heard someone calling my name. I took off my headphones and saw Jose stopping at that light in his truck, waving me over to his window. I ran over to his vehicle, and he asked me what I was doing. I told him I was praising the Lord and getting paid for it. He laughed, wished me well, and the light turned green, so he drove on. The next morning at church, Jose told me that if I wanted, after prayer group, instead of going to day labor, I could come with him and work for his concrete company. I said I would do that. So, instead of leaving with Bobby that morning, I went with Jose, and he took me to a construction site where they were laying steel rebar. He put me out there in the hot sun for my first day on the job. I think I did well that day because he ended up hiring me as a permanent employee. I was excited and earning a lot more money than I did as a day laborer. I performed very well over the next couple of months, and then he promoted me to project manager, along with a raise, a laptop computer, a cell phone, and a company car. Just like that, I had a breakthrough! The lesson here is that if I hadn't listened to the Holy Spirit that day and humbled myself to take the job of flying a sign, I would have missed the blessing God had arranged for me. Later, Jose told me he hired me that day because he thought, "Anyone who would do a job flying a sign in this heat, I could use a guy like that!" Jose became my mentor and discipled me for the next several years while I worked for him, and many years later.

Shortly after receiving my job promotion and being given my company car, I enrolled at Life Christian University and earned my Bachelor of Arts Degree in Theology. I am a licensed and ordained minister, serving as an Evangelist in the fivefold ministry. Now I return to the Texas Prison System, just like all the other men and women prison ministers who poured into me, and I preach the Gospel of Jesus Christ and share my testimony. I witness to prisoners in the same room where I once, as an inmate, lay on the floor on my face, weeping, crying, and surrendering my life to Jesus. Beneath that floor is where my old man is dead and buried, and he is never coming out. When I preach there, I sometimes walk over to that place where I once lay crying, and I jump up and down on that dead man's grave, giving glory to God for transforming me and making me new. Every day now, I have the opportunity to work with drug addicts and those who are incarcerated or just being released from jail or prison, and I am currently mentoring several young men.

Do you remember earlier reading about me trying to jump my car off the 7-Mile Bridge in Florida? Now, let's fast-forward to 2014. I have been released from prison for the second time, and this time I surrendered my life to Jesus. He set me free, and I am loving my new life in Christ. One day, while driving down the highway, I began to feel God's presence with me in the car, and I started to weep. I worshiped Him, praised Him, and shouted out loud that He was so good! Then I heard Him say, "NO MICHAEL, I MADE YOU LIKE THIS!" God waited 17 years to respond to me — shouting out of that car sunroof as I drove through the Florida Keys at 136 MPH back in 1997. God is patient, and His love endures forever. He will never leave you or forsake you; He is with you through good times and bad. I love Jesus. Please give Him a chance to change your life, just as He did mine. If you're mad about your life, you can even yell at God — just don't expect an answer until you're ready to surrender that old life to Him so He can change it!

Jesus has blessed me with a ministry called Sons and Daughters of Thunder that preaches the Gospel of Jesus Christ to those who are struggling with addiction and habitual incarceration, showing them that there is victory over all things in Jesus. The ministry is growing in Texas and other parts of the world. The Lord has also opened doors for me to share the gospel and my testimony with people from different places. About three years after being released from prison, my phone started ringing from an unfamiliar number. It was from a foreign country, and I didn't want to answer it. Then the Holy Spirit whispered to me that I should answer, and I did.

On the other end of the line was Pastor Boimah Duwah from Liberia, West Africa. I didn't even know where Liberia was, and I had no idea why a pastor from Liberia would try to contact me here in the United States. I answered the call, and we started talking. He told me he had read my testimony on Facebook, and it had touched his heart. We talked for a while and shared meaningful conversations about how the Lord found and saved us, making us His disciples. Over the next couple of years, we became friends, communicating through Facebook Messenger and phone calls, and eventually, we grew close. At one point, the pastor told me he was coming to the United States and would be in Dallas, Texas, near where I live, so I decided to meet him. We ended up preaching together at the church, then went to lunch with some church members. During our meal, the pastor from

Liberia invited me to visit his church in Liberia and preach. I excitedly said yes, even though I didn't know the details or how I could get to West Africa. Still, I agreed to come. I just didn't know when.

A few years later, the pastor informed me that a group from Kansas was coming to Liberia for a crusade and revival, and asked if I would join them. I said yes because I was interested in doing this. However, a few days later, while I was in the shower, the Lord spoke to me and told me I wasn't supposed to join the Kansas group; instead, I would lead my own. I said, "Okay, Lord! When the Lord asks me to do something, I do it. I always say yes!" So, I started planning a trip and invited some of the prison ministers who had preached to me while I was in prison to come along on this mission. Pastor Michael Spradlin and Bishop Bruce Bingham joined me on my first trip to Liberia. I was excited to have the chance to do something that felt so adventurous and incredible! I mean, really, "Africa!" This is what an evangelist dreams of his whole life, and now God has called me to Africa. Man, I was pumped! While I was sitting in prison, trying not to use drugs again, I had no idea I would be leading a crusade to preach the gospel in Africa! I promise you, God will blow your mind if you let Him. Your biggest dreams and plans for yourself can't even compare to the plans God has for you.

JEREMIAH 29:11-14 (NIV)

For I know the plans I have for you," declares the Lord, "plans to prosper you and not to harm you, plans to give you hope and a future. Then you will call on me and come and pray to me, and I will listen to you. You will seek me and find me when you seek me with all your heart. I will be found by you," declares the Lord, "and will bring you back from captivity.

As I planned this trip to Africa, Pastor Boimah began to tell me about a group of people in Liberia called the Zogos. I told him,

"Zogos. What is a Zogo?" He said to me," Zogos are the drug addicts in our country. They sit in drug-smokehouses, abandoned buildings, and graveyards, and smoke drugs all day. I thought to myself, 'That's what I used to do.' Then he said, "when the Zogos are out of drugs they go out into the communities. They steal from people and businesses to get money for drugs." I thought to myself again, that is what I used to do. Then I said to the pastor," I am a Zogo." When I said this, he laughed and told me there was no way I was a Zogo. What I did not realize is that nobody would ever claim to be a Zogo because of the stigma attached to that name. A Zogo in Liberia is the lowest person in their society whom the people hate. So, it was very strange for him to hear me claim to be a Zogo. I then told the pastor that when I come to Liberia, I would preach in his church, but only if he would take me to the cemetery and preach to the Zogos. He said to me, "But nobody goes there." I told him that I was going there, and he needed to set it up, and that is what he did. After the five-day revival and leadership conference at the host church, we set up a sound system on the edge of the graveyard and played worship music. Then I began to preach to the Zogos, and they came out of the tombs and crypts of the graveyard, as well as out of the drug smokehouse. They began to praise the Lord. They were begging me to help them because there was nobody who cared about them, and they were dying from this addiction and poverty. I fell in love with them that day because I knew what they were going through, as I too was once like them, hopelessly addicted to drugs. When I first saw the Zogos, I could see myself in them. It was as if I were looking into a mirror. I had so much compassion for them, and their cry was already in my heart. I also knew that I had the answer for their deliverance from drug addiction: Jesus Christ, the Light of the world, who shines in the darkness and the shadow of death. Jesus breaks the chains!

Here is some background information to help you understand what the Lord has called me to do as His disciple. In Monrovia, the capital city, drug addicted men, women, and young people called Zogos have taken over the Palm Grove Cemetery and the Center Street Ghetto at its edge. There are hundreds of tombs in this 13-acre cemetery. Two civil wars from 1989 to 2003 left many bodies to be buried in Liberia. Some of the older drug addicts are the former child soldiers and victims of abuse from this bloody and brutal war, who became addicted to drugs and had nowhere to go when the war was over. The warlords kidnapped the young boys and often killed their family members in front of them, before making them go off to war. To get the frightened children to fight, the warlords gave them drugs to make them brave, and they became addicted. They gave them Marijuana, Cocaine, Heroin, and fed them a mixture of Alcohol, Cane Juice, and Gunpowder that got them high and supposedly made them unafraid. The warlords even made the children cannibalize their victims. Once the disarmament came, the government took away the guns and machetes, but the addiction and trauma stayed. This brutal civil war seeded drug addiction in Liberia, and now there is an entire population of people of all ages addicted to drugs and living in graveyards, swamps, garbage dumps, and ghettos across the country in the most horrible conditions imaginable. The rest of society has forgotten them. They are despised, rejected, and even persecuted by their fellow citizens who hate them. Babies are being born into this environment that never have a chance at a decent life, and the infant mortality rate is high.

In our current times, West Africa continues to serve as an important transit hub for cocaine and heroin coming from the Latin American and Asian producing countries to European markets. This influx of drugs into this region has only exacerbated this overwhelming problem of addiction among the Zogos and Disadvantaged Youth in Liberia, and there are very few resources to help them. These are the hurt, broken, and addicted people of Liberia, and as a disciple of Jesus Christ, God has called me to help them.

The Zogos of Liberia are the despised, rejected, hated castaways, who many believe will never change and will always be criminals and drug addicts. Just like they thought about me when I was hopelessly addicted to drugs, stealing from people and businesses to get high. I have organized a team of both Americans and Liberians, and together we have established a program which is a deliverance, healing, rehabilitation, restoration, and discipleship program for the drug addicted people who live in the streets and tombs of the cemeteries in Monrovia and surrounding areas. Jesus is bringing them out of the drug-smokehouses and tombs by the power of His Holy Spirit. When I am in Liberia, I go into the graveyards, drug houses, and drug huts where they are smoking drugs, and I tell the people inside to put down the drugs, and we begin to worship and praise the Lord. We turn a crack house into a place of worship. We have crusades and revivals where we go to all the ghettos in and around Monrovia and rent buses to pick up all the drug addicts and bring them back to a soccer/football field where we have worship and praise, preach the word, feed the people, give them medical treatment, cut their hair, give them clothes and help them be delivered from the unclean spirit of addiction. The Holy Spirit is so powerful in our services that when I lay hands on people, they fall to the ground, go into seizures, and are delivered. The demons and unclean spirits that these young men and women unwittingly gave access to possess their bodies begin to manifest, and we cast them out in Jesus' name. The evil spirits have no chance of winning when they encounter the power of God. They come out immediately and are cast to the outer darkness and dry places.

It was in Africa for the first time that I realized I was created for spiritual warfare. I received the revelation that I was a soldier of Christ and a warrior for God. The scripture says He trains my hands for war and my fingers for battle. I relate very well to this scripture. I believe that my football career and my 25 years in drug addiction were my training for my Holy War on Addiction. Once I began engaging the enemies of God, I found myself right at home. It's like I am back on the football field, fighting to score and win the game. When I could no longer play football, I was lost and devastated. There was nothing in the world I could find that satisfied me like playing this game. And to me at the time, football wasn't a game. It was life! It wasn't until I entered the battlefield of spiritual warfare in Africa that I found my life again. For 25 years after the game of football ended for me, I travelled the lonely road of drug addiction that led me into complete darkness and into the shadow of death, where I lived. Smoking drugs was my life. In my addiction, I was tormented in my mind and even possessed by demons and unclean spirits. I learned how they operate. I know what they look like and I understand their strategies. I have a thorough understanding of my enemy's strengths and weaknesses. After the anointing, this is what makes me so effective as a Zogo Liberation Freedom Fighter in Africa. It was like God had me doing a special reconnaissance mission into the captivity, darkness and hell of addiction so I could study the enemy so when I engaged the kingdom of darkness in my Holy War on Addiction, I would be ready, prepared, trained up and positioned perfectly to do the most damage possible to win this war as His 6-Star General. I see it all so clearly now! Please understand that everything you have ever gone through, God will use it for the good, from ashes to beauty, and from darkness to light, from utter pain to exceeding glory, from the agony of defeat to the triumph of victory. Make a decision today to see your setbacks as the building blocks to a major comeback in Jesus Christ! Remember, the scripture says that the Lord is a man of war, and since we were created in His image and likeness, that makes us one too. I'm a soldier! I got a sword in my mouth. I preach the gospel, and I kick the devil out. **Stomp the Devil!**

    On one occasion during spiritual warfare, we had an altar call. Pastor Charles Freeman, a large and powerful man, was led to lay hands on a young Zogo man. I was moving through the crowd, praying in the spirit, binding the evil spirits that were in the people. In an instant, I saw Pastor Charles get thrown about ten feet across the altar area, knocking over chairs as he flew by. Then I saw a demon manifesting in a young man. The young man, who was half the size of Pastor Charles, had supernatural strength from the demon. I rushed over to him, but my brother in Christ, Evangelist David Guerra, got to him first. The young man with the demon punched David in the jaw, and then, David and our ministry team wrestled him to the ground. My team had him surrounded, and we were putting a bunch of pressure on him. Then I lay on top of him, calling for the demon to come out.

During the commotion, another Liberian pastor approached the young man and tried to rip a ring off his finger that was given to him by the witch doctor. If we hadn't been there holding him down, that young man and demon would have torn that pastor apart. I rebuked the pastor and told him to step back. I told the pastor that it was not about the ring, but about what was inside the man! After this, I continued praying and commanding the demon to come out. Then I felt a breakthrough, both physically and spiritually. I told everyone to get away from the young man. When I moved away from him, he just lay there in the dirt in the fetal position, curled up like a small ball. He looked like a helpless little child.

I stood over him and helped him to his feet. He looked bewildered, like he had no idea what had just happened. He stood there hunched over, swaying back and forth. At that point, yet another Liberian pastor told me to take his ring off, that it was an evil charm, and the young man wearing it thought it gave him strength. I once again rebuked the pastor and told him that it is not about the ring; it is about what is inside the man.

Then the Holy Spirit told me that this young man would take off the ring and hand it to me himself. When I heard this, I began to tell the young man that I had come all the way from America to help him, but if he wanted my help, he would need to take off the ring and give it to me. I also told him that if he didn't want my help, he could keep the ring on, but he would have to leave. I repeated this about three or four times. Then, after a moment, he stood up, removed the ring, and placed it into my hand. I then told him to take the ring from my hand, throw it on the ground, and step on it. He did exactly that—he took the ring, threw it down, and crushed it into the sand with his foot. I grabbed him and placed his hands over his head, and we began praising Jesus Christ! After a while, I reached back into the dirt, picked up the ring, and threw it as far as I could. When I looked at the ring before throwing it, I saw that it had a marijuana leaf design on its crown. Good-bye forever to that powerless, worthless ring! Praise the Lord!

After the crusade that day, we took the young man to Thunder House. There, we fed him, clothed him, and shaved his head, which is the tradition in Liberia for those who experience a transformation. The next day at the crusade, the young man was part of my ministry team. The following day was Sunday, and the young man attended church with us. The day after that, I baptized him in Jesus' name in the Atlantic Ocean. I am here to tell you, I serve a mighty working God who performs miracles, signs, and wonders.

On another occasion, a young man who was crippled was carried into the altar area during our crusade. The young man was a Zogo, and he was crippled because he was caught stealing, and the community where he was stealing beat him and left him for dead. In Liberia, just like here in the United States, drug addicts steal to pay for their drug habit. As you read in this book, I was a thief to my core and would steal anything from anybody to keep getting high! Well, in Liberia, when a Zogo gets caught stealing, the people will beat him unmercifully, sometimes even to death. It is also known for the community to take a thief and put a tire around him, pour gasoline on him, and set him on fire. The police will not do anything to the people who do these horrible things to thieves. In their culture, they allow for mob justice with no reprisals from the police or government and no prosecution. If they beat a Zogo to death, they put his body in the street, and it lies there for three days for everyone to see and for any of his family members to come and collect it. Then, after three days, the government comes and disposes of the body. Just imagine if it were you who got caught stealing because of your drug addiction, and you lived in Liberia. How many of us reading this book have stolen something because we needed money for drugs? If community members are chasing a Zogo because he has stolen something, he will run to the police station and turn himself in so the community members won't kill him.

Well, in this case, the young man did not die. He was beaten within an inch of his life and lay in the street to die. His friends finally came back to get him and took him back to the smokehouse. For seven months, he was trying to heal, but he was so twisted in pain that he could not walk. Once he was carried to the altar, I saw him and placed my hands on his head, and immediately he fainted and fell to the ground in the spirit. We call it being slain in the spirit. It is when the power of God moves on someone so mightily that it knocks them out and off their feet. They sometimes become unconscious. The young man lay there on the ground, and I began to minister to him and lay hands on him. At one point, I placed my hands on his hips, and I felt the Holy Spirit supernaturally straightening out his body. After a while, he regained consciousness, and I helped him to his feet. The Lord began to heal him, straighten out his legs, and teach him to walk again. Soon, he was up on both feet dancing and praising the Lord for the mighty work He had done. I am a witness of Jesus Christ, and I am here to tell you that as a Disciple of Jesus Christ, you will cast out demons and heal the sick in Jesus' name!

MARK 16:15-18 (NKJV)

And He said to them, "Go into all the world and preach the gospel to every creature. He who believes and is baptized will be saved; but he who does not believe will be condemned. And these signs will follow those who believe: In My name they will cast out demons; they will speak with new tongues; they will take up serpents; and if they drink anything deadly, it will by no means hurt them; they will lay hands on the sick, and they will recover."

Currently, I lead mission trips and organize revivals and deliverance crusades for drug addicts in Liberia, West Africa. I started a ministry in Liberia called Liberation Center Liberia, together with Pastor Sam Nunoo, and we have a dedicated team supporting us on the ground. Liberation Center Liberia offers deliverance, healing, rehabilitation, restoration, vocational training, and discipleship programs for drug addicts who live on the streets, in ghettos, swamps, garbage dumps, drug-smokehouses, and graveyards across Liberia. Our drug rehabilitation discipleship homes are called Thunder House, just as the Lord revealed to me, I would have while I was in prison. I have my old journals from the time I was incarcerated, and I have the entire Thunder House program outlined in those journals. God is so good! I always knew I'd have a drug rehabilitation discipleship program called Thunder House because Jesus told me I would one day. I never thought it would be in Liberia, West Africa—that was a pleasant surprise!

Jesus is saving people from the streets and tombs by the power of the Holy Spirit. We have already built drug rehabilitation discipleship homes called Thunder House. These homes are for men and women who want to be free from drug addiction. We also plan to create a safe home for children of drug-addicted parents. Many children born into addiction are dying, and we are here to help them! In addition to the children's home, we also plan to establish the first Juvenile Boys

Diversionary Discipleship Home. This program will give judges in Liberia an alternative to sending boys to prison with adults. God is blessing the people of Liberia through us!

While I was in Liberia on one of my crusade trips, I met an evangelist who had been a warlord during the Civil War. His name is Joshua Blahyi, but during the wars, he was called "General Butt Naked." Blahyi, as a child, belonged to a people group called the Krahn. The Krahn practiced black magic and believed in child sacrifice. When Blahyi was seven years old, the Krahn elders initiated him as a warrior, and at age eleven, as a high priest. His role as high priest involved overseeing human sacrifices. When the Civil War broke out and a group led by Samuel Doe stormed the capital in a coup d'état, murdered the president and his cabinet, the leader employed Blahyi to perform black magic rituals to help them maintain control of the government. Blahyi later became a warlord, leading a unit of several dozen fighters, mostly child soldiers. They were known as the "Naked Base Commandos" because the only things they wore in battle were their shoes and black magic charms. This is where Blahyi earned his nickname, "General Butt Naked." Blahyi and his child soldiers believed that their dark magic practices made them invisible to bullets. They were also known for engaging in cannibalism of enemies and human sacrifices. His soldiers used alcohol, marijuana, crack cocaine, and heroin to make them fearless, more alert, and more willing to follow his orders. Blahyi claimed that during the fighting, he received a vision from the devil, who told him he would become a great warrior and that practicing human sacrifice and cannibalism would increase his power. Blahyi fought alongside other warlords for control of Liberia's diamond and gold mines so they could trade these resources with drug cartels for weapons and cocaine.

At the end of the war, Blahyi said he had a vision of Jesus Christ and saw the blood of a child on his hands. Jesus asked Blahyi to stop being a slave. After this vision, Blahyi committed his life to Jesus

Christ and became an evangelist, preaching the gospel and helping former combatants come to know the Lord. Pastor Blahyi also runs a program called Journey Against Violence, where he helps young men, women, and ex-combatants break free from drugs and be discipled. I had the honor of having Evangelist Joshua Blahyi preach at our Zogo Liberation Crusade. There, I prayed over him and reminded him that both he and I have always belonged to God and have been His sons and evangelists, even in our darkest moments. We also marched together in one of the Jesus Loves Zogos parades that we hold every year through the streets of Monrovia, the capital city. I was amazed at how he preached and how much the young men and women responded to his words. He and I have become good friends, and every year, my Thunder House Men's team plays his Journey Against Violence Men's team in an exhibition football/soccer match as part of our annual Liberation Cup during our Zogo Liberation Crusade week. His team usually wins, but sometimes we do. Pastor Joshua says his team wins so often because football/soccer is to them like the air they breathe. It's something they can't live without and do constantly. Come on, people! If Jesus can change and redeem a man who was bound like Joshua and turn him into an evangelist and pastor, don't you believe He can change you?

During one of my mission trips to Liberia, we held the Jesus Breaks the Chains Deliverance Crusade. It was a three-day event focused on praise, worship, ministering, feeding, medical treatment, and deliverance from unclean spirits like drug addiction. Before the crusade, during the first two days in the country, we visited prisons in Kakata and at the Firestone Plantation in Harbel. There, we preached and baptized the men and women. On the first day at Kakata, we baptized 95 people, and the next day at Firestone, we baptized another 105 men. Both days were powerful, with men and women crying, weeping, and surrendering their lives to Jesus Christ. Prison conditions in Liberia are horrifying—no electricity or running water, and toilets are just holes in the ground. The stench is overwhelming, and inmates typically receive only one small meal a day, consisting of rice, some gravy, and often chicken necks or feet. Inmates wear their own clothes, as there are no uniforms, and they don't get fresh clothes; they wear what they came in until it wears out. Many prisoners are in poor health, with sores from bed bugs and skin infections due to unsanitary conditions. An important fact to understand is that once you're caught committing a crime in Liberia, you're immediately taken to prison. After the door shuts behind you, it can be two to three years before you see a judge. Those reading this now, in your prison bunk or cell, may not realize how lucky you are. You're living in a luxury hotel compared to your Liberian brothers and sisters in the same situation! So, be grateful for what you have today. Keep things in perspective. I guarantee that your Liberian brothers and sisters locked in those hellish prisons would love to trade places with you right now!

During one of our Zogo Liberation Crusade trips, I was traveling back from the Liberian countryside, and we were passing by one of the largest drug-smoking houses in Monrovia. I told our driver that I wanted to stop and minister to the people there. This place was called Zimbabwe Ghetto, and it had an old abandoned building that the Zogos had taken over, where they smoked drugs day and night. We got out and began ministering to the people there, and the Holy Spirit started to move. As we moved through the crowd outside the smokehouse, the Holy Spirit took control, and we started laying hands on them. They began falling out in the Spirit and being delivered. In Liberia, when this happens, people are slain in the Spirit in a profound way, often becoming unconscious. We spent about 30 minutes doing this outside the smokehouse, then the Lord instructed me to go inside, bind the strong man, and take authority over the smokehouse in His name. I obeyed, went inside, and took authority by binding unclean spirits, demons, and principalities in the spiritual realm, proclaiming God's promises over the drug-addicted Zogos inside. I was overwhelmed in the Spirit. After moving through the smokehouse proclaiming that God would deliver everyone there, I returned to the front porch. I began declaring and decreeing God's Word over everyone present. At that moment, the Liberian Drug Enforcement Agency (LDEA) was approaching the building to raid the smokehouse, but when they saw me on the porch preaching, they turned around and left. The Zogos loved this because, in Liberia, when the LDEA raids a smokehouse, they are very aggressive—they seize whatever money and drugs the Zogos have and sometimes take Zogos to prison. That day, the LDEA did nothing to the Zogos because God had already begun His work through us in the Spirit.

After I finished preaching, I got into the car and we left. Then the Lord began speaking to me and telling me that He wanted me to do the same thing in all of Liberia's drug smokehouses to bind the strongman because He was getting ready to plunder the drug smokehouses, and His plunder was the Zogos who are being held captive there. 'ZOGO LIBERATION IS NOW,' says the Lord! This was when He told me to come back to Liberia and do the same in 70 drug-smokehouses in 7 days.

MATTHEW 12:28-29 (NKJV)
But if I cast out demons by the Spirit of God, surely the kingdom of God has come upon you. Or how can one enter a strong man's house and plunder his goods, unless he first binds the strong man? And then he will plunder his house.

This was when I began planning my November 2024 "70 Smokehouses in 7 Days" Zogo Liberation siege of Liberia's drug smokehouses to bind the strongman so God could plunder the drug smokehouses. You see, the devil stole God's Golden Vessels from God's Temple, and God has commissioned my ministry team and me to go and steal them back for Him. The young men and women who are addicted to drugs and are being hidden in Liberia's drug-smokehouses are going to be liberated and set free. God is going to bring them out of the captivity, darkness, and hell of addiction and deliver them back to Himself and fill them with His Holy Spirit and Fire! Devil be on notice, we are coming for our friends, we are coming for God's gold. And you cannot stop us!

JOEL 3:5-7

Because you have taken My silver and My gold, and have carried into your temples My prized possessions. Also, the people of Judah and the people of Jerusalem you have sold to the Greeks, that you may remove them far from their borders. "Behold, I will raise them out of the place to which you have sold them, and will return your retaliation upon your own head.

I believe God chose this former thief and robber to be a thief and robber for His Kingdom to execute His plan to liberate the Zogos of Liberia from drug addiction and steal them back from the devil and Liberia's drug-smokehouses. I went to prison as a thief and a robber, and when I got out of prison, I was still a thief and robber, except now I "ROB HELL" for Jesus! An interesting thing happened 2 months after I returned home from Liberia, after I bound the strong man in Zimbabwe Ghetto. I read an article online that detailed how the Liberian Drug Enforcement Agency raided the Zimbabwe Ghetto and forced the 100s of Zogos out of it and made the old drug-smoking house a new LDEA office and outpost for their operations. When I read this, the Lord spoke to me and said that the LDEA came to Zimbabwe Ghetto to do this the day I was there, but if they had tried to do it that day, they would have failed. The Lord told me that He sent me there first to do the work in the spiritual realm, to bind the strong man, so that the LDEA could be successful later in the physical realm and drive the Zogos out, and thus God could plunder the smokehouse. All of the Zogos who left the smokehouse that day moved into the tombs of King Gray's graveyard. Since that day, we have rescued many young men from that graveyard and brought them to Thunder House.

I'm also interested in the fact that the only other smokehouse we visited this time in Liberia is the notorious Pelham Building, which is one of the oldest, most prominent, and most well-known drug smokehouses in the country. This smokehouse is located on the edge of Palm Grove Cemetery, on Center Street. It is where I first preached to the Zogos on my first trip. The Pelham Building was the first drug-smoking house ever established by the Zogos in Liberia after the war. They called it Zogo University because that's where you go to learn how to smoke drugs, sell drugs, commit crimes, and be educated and indoctrinated into the Zogo way of life. Two months after we left Liberia, following the strongman's removal, the LDEA moved all the smokers out, and they are not allowed to return. They were pushed back into the graveyard, where they continue to live and smoke drugs today. Because of the dismantling of the two largest and most prominent drug-smokehouses in Liberia, we know that God is true to His Word: "BIND THE STRONG MAN AND PLUNDER HIS HOUSE!" We know firsthand that there is all authority and power in the name of Jesus!

LUKE 10:19 (NKJV)

Behold, I give you the authority to trample on serpents and scorpions, and over all the power of the enemy, and nothing shall by any means hurt you.

In November 2024, I embarked on a siege of Liberia's drug smokehouse, and on November 1, 2024, we began our coordinated attack to bind the strong man of Liberia's drug smokehouses. It was a grueling 7 days of spiritual warfare as we moved through the ghettos, graveyards, swamps, garbage dumps, and abandoned buildings, all used by the Zogos to establish communities and strongholds where they smoke drugs all day and night. It was a great success. We invaded 70 Smokehouse in 7 Days, and on the 7th Day, which was on November 7th, the stronghold of Liberia's smokehouses fell by the Authority and Power of Jesus Christ, and the strongman was bound. Now we continue our plunder of God's Golden Vessels, the Zogos of Liberia.

It is interesting to me that after the "70 Smokehouses in 7 Days" operation, the entire country of Liberia began to collectively take an interest in the drug crisis that started in their country at the end of the civil wars. In 2003, during the disarmament at the end of the war, there were an estimated 80,000 drug users in Liberia, mostly former child and adult soldiers. Twenty years later, in 2023, the Government of Liberia estimated there were over 366,000 drug users. On August 7, 2025, just nine months after "70 Smokehouse in 7 Days," the entire country of Liberia united, and thousands participated in the "Say No to Drugs" march through Monrovia, the capital city. We believe that our work from November 1-7, 2024, opened the gateway from the spiritual realm into the physical realm, allowing heaven to invade earth and giving rise to this movement. Liberia, "Jesus Loves Zogos…Do You?"

The Lord has called me to Liberia to help him set the captives free. To help Him deliver those who are lost in the darkness of drug addiction. I had no idea when I was in prison and surrendered my life to Jesus that I would someday be in Africa doing what I am doing today. That was so far outside of my realm of thinking. Liberia's Zogos are diamonds in the dirt. We need to get down in the dirt and dig them out by the power of the Holy Spirit. We are going into the graveyards and ghettos, snatching young men and women from the devil and stealing them back for God to save them and transform their lives. We are leading the way of Zogo Liberation, carrying the flame that is burning the drug addiction out of Liberia. We are helping God turn drug addicted criminals into Disciples of Jesus Christ. And we do this one soul at a time, in Jesus' Name, by the power of the Holy Spirit!

We have already experienced great success! Liberia's Zogos are overcoming drug addiction and becoming strong men and women of God. They see me as a father figure, and they have given me the nickname "Daddy Zogo." This is one of the highest compliments I've ever received in my life. I love being Daddy Zogo and helping God reclaim the souls that were stolen from Him by the devil. I even have the name tattooed on my chest over my heart to show them that their Daddy always has them on his mind and in his heart, and that I am fighting for them until my last breath. Jesus sacrificed His life on the cross and shed His precious blood so that the Zogo can wear a crown. And I proudly declare, "I am down for the Zogo crown."

It is our duty to fight for this people group known as the Zogo Nation and help them be freed from the captivity, darkness, and hell of addiction, bringing them back to their God. We are at war! This is my mission from God. I received this assignment while I was in prison. I have my marching orders. I wrote a poem about this when I was there, called "HOLY WAR ON ADDICTION." You can read it at the end of this chapter. Yahweh, the Great I AM, has called and equipped me to wage war against the Kingdom of Darkness, to destroy the works of the devil and his weapon of addiction once and for all. This Holy War will be the devil's bitter end!

In March 2025, we held our fourth consecutive Zogo Liberation Crusade, which meant a great deal to me. I was able to take my prison friend, Joshua Culp, also known as "Cellie," to Liberia. When I was released from prison, I said goodbye to Josh and started my new life with Jesus Christ. Josh wasn't as fortunate. When he was released, he returned to his old ways, just like a dog returns to its vomit. Josh was arrested again and ended up behind bars right back at the Travis Unit. One night, I was preaching in the same room where I had surrendered my life to Jesus, and guess who I saw? That's right. My friend and brother, Joshua Culp. When he saw me preaching there, he later told me it gave him hope for the first time in his life that he, too, could be delivered from drugs just like Jesus did with his "Cellie," so he decided to follow my example. He surrendered his life to Jesus, experienced deliverance, and is now being used powerfully by God.

Around the same time, in the same prison and in the same room where I surrendered my life to Jesus, I also met a man named Christopher Pieczynski. It was Chris's ninth time in prison, and he had also been addicted to drugs for over 25 years, just like me. Chris told me that when he heard my testimony, it gave him hope that he, too, could be changed. When he was released from prison, he stayed close to the Lord and followed Jesus as His disciple, and his life was transformed. He became a new creation. After his release, Chris's testimony was featured on "The 700 Club," a Christian television network, and he began serving in prison ministry. Now, Josh, Chris, and I are storming graveyards together in Liberia, West Africa, sharing the love of Jesus Christ with people who are addicted to drugs just like we were before giving our lives to Jesus! Only Jesus can do something like this. God has a plan for your life that you cannot even imagine at this moment. Please surrender your life to Jesus today and let Him do His good work in you. I promise you that you will not be disappointed.

ROMANS 10:10-11 (AMP)

For with the heart a person believes [in Christ as Savior] resulting in his justification [that is, being made righteous—being freed of the guilt of sin and made acceptable to God]; and with the mouth he acknowledges and confesses [his faith openly], resulting in and confirming [his] salvation. For the Scripture says, "Whoever believes in Him [whoever adheres to, trusts in, and relies on Him] will not be disappointed [in his expectations]."

In May 2025, I returned to Liberia to film a documentary about my work with Liberia's Zogos. One of the largest TV producers in the European Union, Arte, produced the documentary "LIBERIA: A PROPHET." This film tells my story—how my journey through the captivity, darkness, and hell of addiction and deliverance back to my God led me to Liberia to combat the country's rampant drug epidemic. Our ministry, Liberation Center Liberia, has declared a Holy War on Addiction. We are taking the fight to the enemy and going into the places where people use drugs—snatching those souls and bringing them into our drug rehabilitation discipleship program so their lives can be transformed forever. Our battle cry is "JESUS LOVES ZOGOS," and we are sharing the love of Jesus Christ with those addicted to drugs living in graveyards, swamps, garbage dumps, and drug smokehouses across Liberia. Thank you to the most talented and creative filmmakers in the world: Maxime Priou, Arthur Rayssiguier, and Pierre Chabert. The documentary release date is October 2025, and it will be available on YouTube (www.youtube.com/c/ARTEDocumentary), the Arte website (www.arte.tv/en), and other streaming services. A highlight for me will be attending the premiere screening of the film in Paris, France, with my daughter, Brooke. My daughter told me recently that I am her best friend. Only Jesus can do a restoration like this.

My message to every drug addict, incarcerated person, or anyone who is not living out their purpose in God is that Jesus has an incredible life for you if you ask Him into your heart, repent of your sins, and confess Him as the Lord and Savior of your life. Let His light shine in your darkness and the shadow of death where you now sit. That is the reason why He came into this world. The devil is a liar, and he is already defeated, and so is your addiction. Jesus has triumphed in victory over all things, and now you must enforce that victory by making Him the Lord and Savior of your life! Do it now!

LUKE 1:79 (NKJV)

To give light to those who sit in darkness and the shadow of death, To guide our feet into the way of peace."

I am here to encourage you, whoever you are. God has big plans for you—to become His disciple and to live a life of Victory, Strength, Purpose, and Hope. A crack house, a prison cell, falling down drunk next to your toilet in your bathroom, smoking drugs in the tombs of a graveyard, or sitting in an alleyway with a needle in your arm is not your end. God has more for you than that if you trust Him and surrender your life to Him completely, just as I have done. You are called to be a child of God—children of the light, children of the day! Designed to become workers in His fields of harvest for lost souls. An offspring of servant-workers with a purpose to take Jesus into all the world and shine His light in the darkness and shadow of death. He chooses us, who have been rescued from the darkness, to return filled with the Light of Jesus Christ to help bring others out. We come out of the darkness to help with God's harvest. He chooses us because He knows He can trust us and that we are not afraid of the darkness. We are His warrior clan, sent into the battlefield to advance His Kingdom! Awake and rise, and be delivered from your addictions. Be filled with the Holy Spirit, Fire, and Power, and share your testimony with everyone you meet about how Jesus changed you when you surrendered your life to Him. You were created for a time such as this. You are a chosen one to be enlisted in His end-time army. It is a time of dominion—a war for ancient thrones! We win this war on drug addiction one soul at a time, in Jesus' name! You are that one!

1 THESSALONIANS 5:5-9 (NIV)
You are all children of the light and children of the day. We do not belong to the night or to the darkness. So then, let us not be like others, who are asleep, but let us be awake and sober. For those who sleep, sleep at night, and those who get drunk, get drunk at night. But since we belong to the day, let us be sober, putting on faith and love as a breastplate, and the hope of salvation as a helmet. For God did not appoint us to suffer wrath but to receive salvation through our Lord Jesus Christ.

The Lord has called me out of this world, addiction, and habitual incarceration into Him and the Spirit of Truth, commissioning me to spread His Word to those still lost and living in defeat, showing them that there is Victory in our Lord and Savior Jesus Christ. This is my charge! Praise God, for He is my "Everything," and I am His witness that He saved me from the captivity, darkness, and hell of addiction by His Mighty Right Hand! There is only One God, and His name is Jesus. He is an awesome God, a good God, and I want to share Him with others who are in bondage to addiction, prisons, or anything preventing them from living their purpose in Him. I found true freedom in the most unlikely place—prison—when I surrendered all to Jesus! You, too, can find freedom from whatever has you bound by surrendering your life to Jesus, as I have done. In Jesus Christ alone, I have finally found the success I had always sought in this world but could never seem to find. I have finally been set free.

Jesus Breaks the Chains...
"Who the Son Sets Free Is Free Indeed"
Michael Bowen, you are Free!

HOLY WAR ON ADDICTION

Bronze bow
Bent on danger
Down my arm
Pointed at the stranger
As David lived
I too am a man of war
Charging hard at the enemy
Always wanting more
I am the way
The way of the arrow
I fly by sight
With eyes of the sparrow
My aim is focused
Like a straight shooting dart
A blazing fire
Burning in my heart
The battle has formed
Flying arrows turn day into night
Pointed tip laced
Covered in light
The serpent slivers
Slicing from his pit
Fire of his own
Ready to spit
His venom full
Deception and lies
The battle is fought
For spiritual lives
My arms are strong
And so is my mind
I am with Jesus

I crossed that line
His mighty Army
The rest left to death
My arrow flies straight
To the enemy's chest
Holy War On Addiction
Sons and Daughters of Thunder combined
Taking the fight to the enemy
We hold the line
Jesus has shouted
His warrior's cry
We never surrender
We never quit
We never die
Death has been swallowed
As Victory licks its lips to taste
Holy War on Addiction
The enemy knows his true place
Jesus has conquered
And sits in His rightful seat
Addiction, the devil, all enemies
Get under our feet
We are His Army
The marching of the Saints
Holy War On Addiction
Precious Blood Painted Face
We are Holy Warriors
Coming to cash in
We are coming for our gold
We are coming for our friends
I am the arrow
Pulled from the quiver of my Lord
My target is addiction
I am wielding a Mighty Sword

Addiction be on notice
The enemy and his friends
Sons and Daughters of Thunder are coming
This Holy War will be your bitter end!

MY LIFE

My life
The American dream
From rags to riches
Hopes turned into means
Money came quick and easy
Fame from the gifted athlete in me
Lifestyles of the rich and famous
Where will all the good times lead
The end has always been a question
Blinded by the happenings in between
Just around the corner speeding
An unsuspecting wall of disaster unseen
Into the world of addiction crashing
Fueled by my life's money and success
Something had to come and balance
This shooting star on his victory quest
My life has been a roller coaster
Up and down with pride and shame
My life has been a river
Emptying into the ocean of guilt and blame
My life has been a mountain
Always climbing to the top
Lifting my arms in victory
Then falling down the other side on slippery rocks
My life has been a journey
Into addiction a tormenting flame
A furnace of affliction
Bound by heavy oppression in chains
The ups and downs have wearied
The toll on this man has always been steep
The payment cost me everything

Head covered by water sinking into the deep
Stranded in the pit of my addicted hell
Rebelliously filling my insatiable appetite for the drugs
Wickedness seeding in me its garden
Its weeds trying to choke out the last of my love
My life once again has fallen
From on high it has fatally dropped
Sitting amongst the living dead
In my tracks this speeding train has suddenly stopped
Pride and wealth are no longer
Long gone all the fortune and fame
Seeing the end is now in question
Nowhere else to look but into the mirror for something to blame
This man has always been quick to compromise
My soul for the acquisition of promising worldly things
This world has found itself another sucker
Its riches I thought happiness they would bring
In this land of broken promises
Another dark valley of bones do I sit
Searching for truth and some answers
Forgiveness for my sins I hope to get
The path to the top was always glorious
Feeding off my hard work in the climb
Looking to the day of my bright future
Once I reached the pinnacle and could shine
With the last step to the top, I was grateful
Perseverance always carried me to the peak
I raised my arms in victory
Excitement in the words did I speak
Cheering crowds once again I had imagined
High fives and fist pumps that wouldn't quit
There I believed I would be happy
In triumph on my throne, I thought I would sit
Accomplishments are this world's currency

Its gold is hey would you look at me
Having found my way again to the top of success
What was it that I was supposed to see?
It looked like the same old environment
Feelings of failure still tugging at me
Always at the top was disappointment
Still unable to shake myself free
I always felt like a misfit
Why is this process not working for me?
I've seen it work for all the others
A lesson in life instilled early on in this successful man someday I would turn out to be
My life has always been a confusing puzzle
Trying to fit a square peg into a round hole
Like a man swimming through muddy river
Trying to find a quenching for his thirsty soul
Like a fish out of water
To this world I always tried to be another king
Like an angry dog chasing cars
This world's promises I thought joy they would bring
Now I know I am different
Chosen by God out of this world before time began
Made sick by belief in this world's systems
Healed by the precious blood of the lamb
Today I stand humbled at the bottom
Rejuvenated spirit, delivered soul and recaptured sober mind
I rest easy in Christ Jesus
In Him real success I did find
True riches are found in the spirit
On the wings of His Mighty Grace, I now fly
High above all this world's mountains
No longer tricked into having to climb
From rags to riches now has new meaning
So too does the story of my life

In Christ Jesus I have found eternity
In eternity there is no end in sight
Jesus is my Holy Mountain
In Him from far above this fallen world I now see
The journey of mine through the fires of addiction
The only way this man could ever truly be set free

HIS BRAND

Sideways running from something
Down another mountainside of slippery rocks
Being chased by the shadows of evil
Broken heart pounding unable to stop
Startled by every movement of the wind
Pursued patiently by the approaching unseen
No time to think out loud
My mind overflowing awake with broken dreams
No map to follow my future
All bridges crossed have been tragically burned
Running into my addicted darkness
A stomach wretched in fear violently churns
What a lonesome sad feeling heightened
Charged by the quick escape into the unknown
Adrenaline has now made its appearance
The maniac hiding in me again has found itself a home
My body pricked in false excitement
Fueled by the surge of mounting fear
Running fast in a race with the enemy
Like fighting through smoke nothing is clear
Landscapes of mountains before me
Not enough strength right now for a new climb
Dark valleys travel more easily
Trying to keep hidden from the beast that seeks to find
Running into a mirror backwards
Chasing my fleeing self
Like a gecko in imminent danger
To all reality I have made myself stealth
Unable to approach understanding
Wisdom so far out of my reach
I have fallen again into the warzone

The enemy my fortress has breached
The high walls I had erected
Have come crumbling down around my falling tower of pride
Now I am sent fleeing into nothing
Nowhere to stop, nowhere to rest, nowhere to hide
Once I was sure in my own reason
So sure of the iron clad life I had built
Now I am left running from shadows
Like a roughed up pinball machine I have gone full tilt
Hopefully I can soon realize
This maniac running blindly through insanity is headed for a wall
Out of control speeding locomotive
Crazy train down the hill no brakes after a fall
Nothing can be accomplished by continuing to run
The enemy pursuing is the addiction that has been secretly seeded in me
The drugs no longer moving me fast enough
Slowing me down so prey I can be
Set myself up for fail once again
The cunning enemy with its deceptions and lies
Feeding on the desires of my flesh
Taken once again by its forgetful disguise
Addiction always comes knocking
On a door I have conveniently left unchained
Addiction with its own quiet whispers
Only I can be left to blame
Same old inflated story
Addiction saying I will show you a better way
Locked in your fortress soul divided
Come with me and we'll run away
This place has you continually baffled
Look at all the good you have already done
No one appreciates the hard work you do
You really do owe yourself some fun

Remember all the excitement
Way back when we used to play
Let's go back to that time
We can do it all again like that today
Once again I believe the fantasy
Like a great movie with a happy storybook ending
My mind has skyrocketed into the cosmos
My addictive thoughts the truth it is happily bending
Now I look back behind me
Stopping for just a second to catch my breath
Hiding myself amongst the thorny chaos
The sharpness of the briars warning me of death
Peeking back at my escaped reality
Only walls of this dark pit do I see
Yes again I have fallen greatly
The fires of my addicted hell laughing at me
Flames of angry torment
Sharp points of confusion they do strike
Never have I fallen this deeply
Demons biting feeding on the last of my light
Crying out for anything to save me
Hoping to be heard by my almost forgotten God
Drowning alone at the bottom in misery
Time nearing an end with an evil nod
For me as I am a witness
For me this lost child of Almighty God
For me lost in the captivity, darkness and hell of addiction
Long ago I was promised by His Word the protection of His staff and his rod
Suddenly I feel a presence
Out of nowhere comes a familiar trusted hand
My God reaches in to save me
Jesus plucks from the fire this brand
Like Joshua in the vision of Zechariah

Satan standing by admiring his fine work
God faithfully delivers me His child to freedom
From captivity, darkness and hell addiction had took
Standing on His rock in filthy garments
Jesus holding my still shaking hand
God comforts and clothes me in wisdom
Shows me in my own vision a new promised land
Thus sayeth the Lord unto me
If you will walk in obedience and hold true to my ways
If you will keep my commands and requirements
I will give you a place to stand tall the rest of your days
God spoke to me my new mission
Still flaming out of the fire in His hand my charge He gave
Now you will go back into addiction
From the foundation of this rock you will help others from the same dark fiery grave
Now I am in full preparation
God seeding His life-giving word in me
Becoming my refuge, my fortress, my high tower
Gaining strength this mighty Warrior of God to be
God uses a fiery furnace
For me it was addiction that lit fire to this brand
Like gold purified and steel made stronger
In Christ Jesus a righteous vessel I now stand
Standing tall upon His Holy Mountain
Faithful tree now bearing His good fruit
My feet shod firmly on His rock
The Gospel of Peace now I do preach
Holy War on Addiction
Sons and daughters lost in foreign lands
Call out from your own pits for your Savior
Be plucked out of your fiery addiction for you too are His Brand
You are His precious children
Into captivity blindly you have been led

Through many lies and deceptions
For much too long you have been fed
Turn off the running water
Keeping you comfortable in the enemy's hand
Let the heat move you to wisdom
Be delivered from the horrible pit you now stand
Addiction will always keep you falling
Deeper and deeper into guilt and shame
Tormenting lies into confusion
Only you have you to blame
All the wrong decisions
Bad choices at every turn
Quick to take the easy road travelled
Now in the pit you continue to burn
Reach out for the hand that is extended
The mighty right hand of the Most High God
Be plucked from the fire His Brand
On His rock your feet will be shod
Healing will take time from the damage
No damage is ever much too severe
Jesus Christ is the hand that saves you
It is His voice of Truth you now faithfully hear
He has come to comfort you gently
To heal you back to a new way of life
God always plucks His lost children
Always saving us by His loving light
Since before you were born you have been His Brand
Into this world and many fires you have never been alone
Finally the time has come to collect you proven
In Christ Jesus you have finally come home
We are God's chosen brand for His fire
To light up this wicked world in us He placed His spark
Red hot blazing fiery brand pulled from the furnace
Flaming torch leading us out of the dark

We are His precious children of light
Jesus Christ at the right hand our Mighty King
Setting on fire His creation boldly through us
The reason out of the fire His brand, YOU!...He does bring!

MIRRORS

Staring into a mirror
Startled by the stranger looking back at me
Unfamiliar eyes unfocused
Something has stolen who I used to be
Once there was a light
Now just a dark stranger invading my space
Eyes once full of excitement
Now just a cracked mirror broken face
What have I become
When will I be able to shed this evil disguise
Who is this lonesome nobody
Why all the sadness filling his eyes
Reflections in a mirror
This stranger just an illusion from the other side
Wickedness attacks through smoked filled rooms
My terrorized spirit retreats somewhere to hide
Our eyes are the windows of our souls
As a child of light lost I am confused by the dark
Looking into this mirror
I expected to see that same old familiar spark
Bright lively eyes once framed by truth
Now replaced by dark eyed cold lying stare
This mirror I have found is a deceiver
An illusion telling me I am no longer there
Continuing down this path gone crooked
My lost feet still stepping along this unfamiliar way
This road I have travelled has led me into destruction
The cost of the damage to my soul I am unable to pay
My spirit has been compromised
Crying out to be delivered from all the pain
Reaching through smoke grasping for freedom

Desperately trying to find a way out of this wicked game
Mirrors in all directions
Looking for the one reflecting the good light
All others are leading to the same wall of darkness
There is only one way to get back my good sight
Mirrors are on the move everywhere
Mirrors with many reflections on the go
In one of them I hope to find myself
In that good mirror my face has to show
Searching for my lost mirror
Two mirrors face off reflecting the unseen
The image unlocked leads deep into eternity
Time and space here are thrown away into a dream
Mirror reflecting mirror
The reflection of a reflection that never ends
Head first dive into forever's reflection
I am now off on my journey to find my lost friend
Stepping into my future brightly
Tip toeing gracefully across a beam of reflective light
Now I see my spirit in hiding
Out of the blind dark eternity has given me back my good sight
Back to my future in the present
Eternity has helped me uncover never-ending power and grace
In a tide pool hidden behind the rocks in a river of living water
In beauty I see my face reflecting my face
God has created us in His image
We were made by Him to always reflect His everlasting light
Like mirrors taken up by the wind
Our spirits were born to forever be in flight
Always free from the captivity of darkness
Flying high above the heaviness of this earth
Dancing in sweet rhythm across the clouds
Each new day in Christ Jesus brings rebirth
We are born of flying spirit

Delivered on the wings of God's amazing grace
Once we look away from His love
The mirror we trust will quickly be replaced
God says if you seek Me
Come after me with all of your might
You will find your good reflection in My son
I will deliver you from the darkness of your night
I am God over all creation
My son Jesus the Christ is your King
Our love reflects in all directions
It is the eternal song now your spirit happily sings
You are my treasured possession
Created as a reflection of me for all creation to see
We are each other's mirror
Face to face only in Christ Jesus we will always be
Look into the light on focus
Your spirit feeding on the bread of life in the Word
I look through you when you look at yourself
When you join our song it makes the sweetest music ever heard
Staring into a mirror
In Christ Jesus once again I see my beautiful self
Never again will I trust other mirrors
No longer will my spirit have to go stealth
Looking back to my future now in the present
God's eternal light a reflection to all through me
This child of light has found his way home
My journey into eternity through my good reflection I now see

MY NEW SONG

Music streaming backwards
This wicked song to sing
Dancing in addicted darkness
Only more drugs my sideways calling does bring
Serving the air in ignorance
Blinded by smoke wisps and hot fire stares
No measure can take me far enough
Shot out of a cannon with no cares
My arms torn in a dogfight
Kamikaze pilot flying into an already sinking ship
Sharp teeth biting into confusion
Bleeding heart at the end of my broken tip
Broken too is this vessel
Cracked by the fall into this pit
My future is still falling
Wobbling legs unable to sit
Reaching blindly into the darkness
Bloody fingers tearing at a circle of walls
Unable to find understanding
Kicking open the bathroom stall
Running wild into the open
Fueled by the white lightning in the ice
Sleeping with my eyes wide open
Going out of business sale with no price
Nothing left to hold onto
No more gas left in the tank
Beam me up again scotty
Like hunting lions with a gun full of blanks
To make sense of nothing is useless
My worthless word has no value at all
Last dollar bill in quarters

Like old cartoons follow the bouncing ball
This is my melody of sound reason
Addiction's sad lonesome highway song
Follow the ball for hours
All the right lyrics are wrong
Spinning around on the turntable
The broken record keeps skipping a beat
The needle has sharpened in lopsided rhythm
The song never sounded so bitter sweet
Music streaming backwards
In traffic the sounding of honking horns
Racing to by another broken record
In my future just another one of many storms
Raindrops falling on my windshield
Speeding car lost with no brakes
Driving me deeper into addicted darkness
Every cell in my body aches
Every thought in my mind still confusion
The dead end in sight an unforgiving wall
I take my foot off of the gas pedal
Hoping the engine will fatally stall
Something has come to trigger
The lion laughs at the gun in my hand
The bouncing ball has suddenly stopped jumping
The hour glass has just run out of sand
Time has come to a standstill
The car out of gas has rolled to a stop
The turntable has stopped spinning
So quiet as the pin drops
Music is no longer streaming backwards
The ship hit the bottom of the sea
Today is the day I stop using
This is the day finally I am free
Now that the evil song has ended

Enters the stage a beautiful light
No more dancing in darkness
An end to all no return flights
Now my legs no longer wobble
Standing firm no smoke in sight
The only measure now is my freedom
As I look into my future I see everything will be alright
Sweet song playing on the radio
Open road driving without all the sudden stops
Headed for today's destination
Full tank of gas rear view mirror no cops
Headed for a beautiful reunion
Down the road to be with my own
Soon I will be holding my children
Tears in my eyes as they have grown
Its been over a year since I have seen them
Much too long to have been away
I hope they can somehow forgive me
My new song to them starts today!

JESUS IS THE CURE

Addiction is a cancer
A plague and destroyer from within
A common cold
Quickly to set in
Feeding on your light
Blood stained in the end
A life entangled in a noose
A soul chained to sin
Always waiting for an answer
To questions without end
Unable to understand
The unfaithfulness of a friend
Addiction is always calling
The spirit always pushed out
An ancient decision
A new way has been found
Addiction is planted
Seeds of wickedness sown
Evil spirits hidden in the drugs you use
The effects will grow unknown
An addict to be discovered
Will always arrive unawares
Will fall hard for the deception
Exciting fun was the snare
Once caught with a smile
The trap closes its grip
Now the game has changed
The addict put on the tip
The point of all confusion
A steady stream of lies
Unending sorrow

Flood of tears fill the eyes
Broken heart no surrender
No white flag in this sad song
Addiction is a journey
The way very long
Only to capture the moment
The day the lie is found out
Addiction can be destroyed
Call for Jesus with a shout
Scream for your savior
Yell for your soul is in doubt
Be plucked from your hell
For only Jesus is the way out
Salvation for all is now
For you the addict it is today
Ask Jesus to be the Lord of your life
Only then can you be saved
Be baptized in repentance
In the water you shall lay
Be filled with the Holy Spirit
His Fire will burn your addiction away
Praise His Holy Name daily
For praise will stand the test
In Christ Jesus there is no addiction
In Him the cure is His rest
Addiction in you no longer remains
In its place now you are blessed
Jesus is the cure
In Christ Jesus you are your very best!

If this story touched your heart and you would like to partner with Michael Bowen and his ministry in Texas, USA, and Liberia, West Africa, you can do so by making a financial donation at the following websites:

www.sonsanddaughtersofthunder.org
www.liberationcenterliberia.org

Or you can give by check at the following address:

SDT Ministries
1841 S. Lakeline Blvd. Suite 101-131
Cedar Park, TX 78613

Or through **CashApp** at: Or through **Venmo** at:
$SDTLCL   **@Michael-Bowen-0014**

Sons and Daughters of Thunder Ministries is a Texas, USA 501 (c) (3) Non-Profit Corporation, and Liberation Center Liberia is a registered Not-for-Profit Liberian NGO, and all donations will receive a receipt for tax purposes wherever applicable.

Sow a Seed into **Sons & Daughters of Thunder Liberation Center Liberia**, to fulfill God's mission and vision both locally and globally.

God blesses us so we can be a blessing to others. He provides for this ministry through your generosity, and we thank you—you are truly making a difference. The Word of God says it is better to give than to receive, and you will reap what you sow! We truly appreciate your giving and sowing.

Luke 6:38 (NKJV)
Give, and it will be given to you: good measure, pressed down, shaken together, and running over will be put into your bosom. For with the same measure that you use, it will be measured back to you."

Made in the USA
Coppell, TX
19 January 2026

68405817R00132